HAMMER

&

N
A
I
L

Important Safety notice

Using a saw and/or hammer to work with wood and other
materials inherently includes the risk of injury and damage.
We cannot guarantee that creating the projects in this book is
safe for everyone. For this reason, this book is sold without
warranties or guarantees of any kind, expressed or implied,
and the publisher and the author disclaim any liability
for injuries, losses or damages caused in any way by the
content of this book or the reader's use of tools needed to
complete the projects presented herein. The publisher and the
author urge readers to thoroughly review each project and to
understand the use of all tools before beginning any project.

Making and assembling furniture designs
inspired by Enzo Mari

HAMMER

&

N
A
I
L

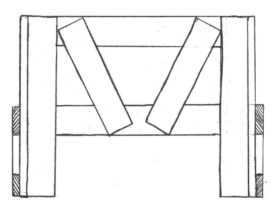

Erik Eje
Almqvist

Photography by Hilda Grahnat

PAVILION

Introduction
9

Never satisfied:
Enzo Mari
and contemporary design
15

Read this
chapter before
you start
27

Furniture

Introduction

A few years ago, I came across a spiral-bound book with black-and-white pictures and assembly plans for building furniture using nails and standard timber. The furniture was distinctively simple; the pine timber was untreated, the heads of the nails visible and the saw cuts unsanded.

At the same time, the pieces were clever, comfortable and harmonious. They didn't hide anything – on the contrary, they seemed to consciously show off how they were assembled. Looking at them was like taking a basic course both in structural design and ergonomics.

The book, *Autoprogettazione?,* was written in 1974 by the Italian designer Enzo Mari. When I read about him, the image of a white-bearded and uncompromising radical, who seemed to be filled by equal amounts of a creative drive to work and antipathy towards modern culture, took shape. He had created an eclectic range of award-winning products: a rocking steel tray, an animal-shaped wooden puzzle, a plastic wall calendar, a bin that tilts so that it's easier to score a three-pointer with your scrunched-up paper...

In old TV interviews, he chews on expensive cigars as he categorically proclaims the spiritual death of Western civilization. He laments that the role of the designer has been reduced to creating vacuous decorations that barely fulfil a function beyond keeping up consumption in a market that continuously demands new products.

Mari was 42 when he wrote the little pamphlet with furniture plans. It was a clear act of protest. A kind of anti-design in reaction to the method of working where each object in turn is designed, marketed and sold. Mari instead gave his plans away for free to anyone who sent a stamped addressed envelope to his office on Piazzale Baracca in Milan.

Many interpreted the book as a manifesto of nostalgic longing for a pre-capitalist society where people built what they needed themselves, but Mari's goal wasn't to make people cease consuming. Rather, he wanted to make them consider the more basic aspects of the objects we surround ourselves with. What is a piece of furniture? What makes it beautiful? Comfortable? Functional? And why do we buy the interior objects that we do? The plans were, he wrote, a way to encourage people to practise 'thinking with their hands'.

Personally, when I unearthed a copy of *Autoprogettazione?*, I felt like I had struck gold. My family and I had just moved and money was running short. With these plans, I could furnish a whole home.

Unfortunately, the measurements in the book weren't very clear. The Italian translation was cryptic and, since they have different timber dimensions in Italy, the plans didn't correspond to the timber that was sold where I'm from in Sweden.

I therefore started to adapt several of Mari's plans to work with standard boards, although as mentioned standard boards might not be the same measurements in all countries so please do check and adjust if necessary. During the work it became clear that all his furniture followed certain principles – right-angle cuts, overlapping and visible joints, measurements and angles strictly tailored according to the human anatomy.

I designed some of my own furniture following the same basic principles. Eventually the idea to turn the work into a book started to take shape, and I was given permission from Mari's publisher to publish my adapted plans of his furniture. The result is not a book for advanced furniture makers. On the contrary, I want to encourage everyone to pick up a hammer. The projects and the methods described are so simple that anyone and everyone should be able to put them together successfully.

In a time when people who dedicate their free time to cycling or cooking, for example, are expected to buy professional equipment and invest in hand-forged chefs' knives, I also want to make the case for daring to be a simple amateur with a hobby. You neither have to buy expensive tools nor dedicate yourself to learning ancient Japanese joinery methods to be able to build your own furniture.

It's satisfying to dine at a table that you have built yourself. But to learn basic carpentry for your household needs can also be a way to free yourself from the notion that making is something that only craftsmen do and that your only option is to consume.

In the great Enzo Mari's words: The only way to avoid being designed is to create yourself.

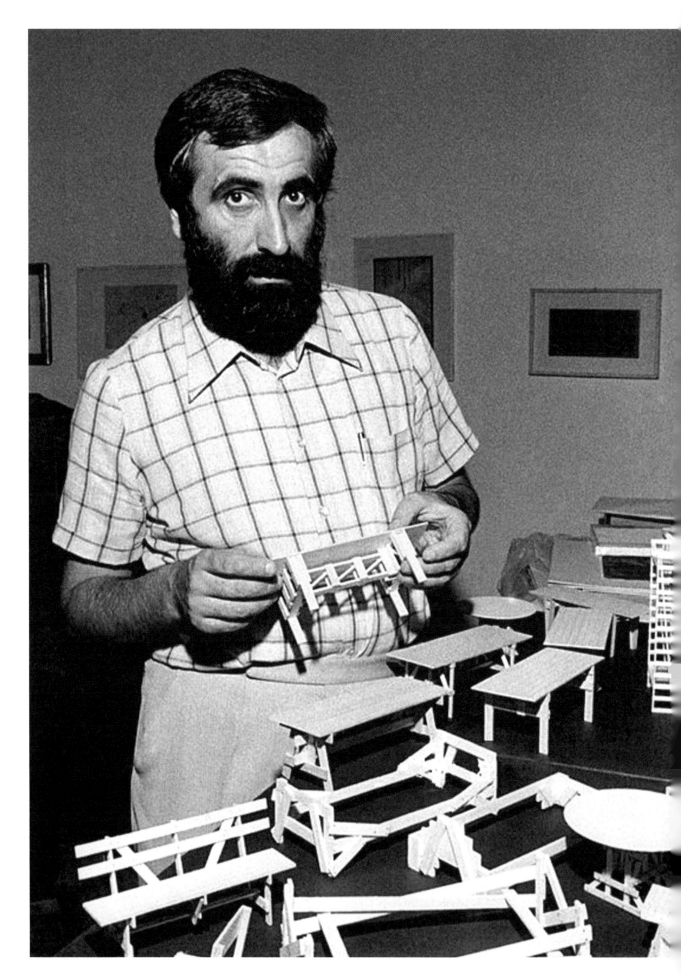

Never satisfied: Enzo Mari and contemporary design

In 2006, Enzo Mari was invited to lecture at the prestigious Serpentine Gallery in London. The mood among the architects, journalists and design students that had assembled in the lecture hall was one of excitement. The white-bearded designer might not have been as much of a household name as Man Ray, Jean-Michel Basquiat, Zaha Hadid and the other superstars whose work had been shown at the Serpentine, but within the trade, the Italian was renowned. For over 50 years he had created everything from plastic citrus squeezers and clever wooden toys, to modernist steel chairs that had become a part of MoMA's permanent collection in New York. His creations, motley in form, were united by an uncompromising construction theory. Mari proclaimed that a designer's foremost task is to create practical solutions that improve people's lives, and he was convinced that every useful object has an ideal design. With his explicit aversion to decorations and market adaptations he had become a kind of trade conscience – the intellectual designers' designer.

However, the lecture didn't become the retrospective review of Mari's work and theories that most had expected. It was as if the context itself annoyed him. He had barely introduced the lecture before he worked himself up so much that he diverged from the main topic and started ranting about things that he abhorred.

He declared that the design industry was essentially dead and that his colleagues mostly spent their time interpreting trends and producing 'nice products' instead of finding creative solutions to real material and philosophical problems. 'Everything is pure shit.' *Merda pura.*

Mari, an outspoken communist, continued to reject contemporary architecture and all of Western civilization on the whole. When he spotted the world-famous Dutch architect Rem Koolhaas in the audience, who had created the Serpentine's pavilion that year he denounced him as 'a pornographic window dresser'.

As Koolhaas, all dressed in black, shook his fist, Mari went on to dissect other aspects that had gone wrong in the fabric of capitalist society. Afterwards the design critic Alice Rawsthorn asked him: 'Is there any aspect of contemporary life that pleases you?' Mari was quiet for a long time. Then he answered:

'Bread and terrorism.'

'Why terrorism?' asked Rawsthorn.

'Why not?' answered Mari. 'People think it's bad but if they thought about it, they'd realize it isn't all bad. It changes things.'

One way to look at Enzo Mari is as the design world's equivalent to Larry David's eponymous character in the TV series *Curb Your Enthusiasm*. A person with a pathological inability to keep quiet as soon as the social norms start to ring just the slightest bit false. Who, instead of accepting the situation and adapting accordingly to the circumstances, seemed convinced that he'd be able to persuade his fellow human beings to change.

This behaviour, of course, often led to great

disappointment. The fact is that Mari's whole career has followed a steady rhythm where time after time he has torn down what he has built up for himself: three step forwards and two steps back.

It was far from given that Luigi and Carolina Mari's eldest son should study. Luigi didn't have an education and managed to scrape along as a handyman. In 1915 he had travelled over 600 miles on foot from his childhood home in Apulia, on the heel of Italy, to Novara, just to the west of Milan. Here he met Carolina and a son was born. The boy was regarded as gifted and, when he was old enough, they enrolled him at secondary school where he studied art history. But, when Enzo was 14, his father became so ill that he could no longer work. The responsibility to support the family fell to Enzo, who quit school and started to work selling goods.

Every morning and evening when Enzo went out to work, he saw the students at the nearby art school walking past with their canvases. He bought his own brushes and applied himself, spending his free time ploughing through thick academic books on art history that he didn't understand.

After four years selling his wares, he applied to the art school himself. When he at last got to study painting, sculpture and interior design, he was so full to bursting with questions that the teachers repeatedly asked him to leave the classroom so as to not disturb the lesson. Soon he switched to a course in psychology and eventually dropped out of school altogether. However, even without a degree he still managed to convince the newly started furniture company, Danese, to produce a squiggly wooden puzzle with outlines of 16 animals that could be combined in different ways.

The puzzle, which became an unexpected hit, was followed by a picture book. *La Mela e la Farfalla* (*The Apple and the Butterfly*) would make toddlers question what the caterpillar did in the cocoon and start reflecting on the cycle of life. This also became a success. But when Mari delivered the sequel *L'Uovo e la Gallina* (*The Egg and the Chicken*), the publisher thought he had gone too far in his pedagogic ambitions. They couldn't publish a book aimed at children that with 'pornographic detail' described how an egg was fertilized. Mari, who thought he had already censored himself in the production of the cockerel and the hen's mating act, refused to compromise further.

During the sixties, Mari designed several products that made the most of the possibilities of plastic and aluminium for producing cheap, durable and flexible furniture. He started teaching at prestigious schools and, in 1972, when MoMA in New York, he arranged a large exhibition about the innovative, cutting-edge design of post-war Italy, Mari and a few of his fellow countrymen were invited to show their work. When the exhibition opened, the podiums gleamed with plastic and chrome. Mari, however, chose instead to contribute an essay in which he argued for the designer's role in class struggle, and questioned the ethics of the very idea of designing products that were to be sold to a consumer.

In the early seventies, Mari suffered from depression triggered by a sofa bed. It started when the furniture producer Driade asked whether Enzo Mari could design this type of product for them.

Mari saw the offer as a chance to make a difference. All the sofa beds he had seen were 'vulgar, obscene and surgically complicated to transform from sofa to bed'. But people living in cramped accommodation were just as much in need of good furniture as those who were well off. He created a pared-back bed with curved steel legs. The cylindrical back rest could easily be folded backwards. Mari confirmed proudly that the construction was simple enough to be sold cheaply, but sturdy enough to sleep two people.

Ten thousand Day-Night sofa beds were produced – but it was a commercial flop. When the producer later scrapped the unsold sofas, they assessed what had gone wrong. According to the analysis the sofa bed had been *too* cheap: customers in the target market dreamed of waterbeds and marble, they would rather have furniture that symbolized their aspirations than furniture that simply fulfilled their needs.

Mari became so depressed by the conclusion that he considered changing profession. If he was just making things that no one understood, he might as well pack it all in. But then an idea came to him, an idea that in hindsight seems very Enzo Mari. If he could get people to build and design furniture themselves, perhaps they would understand the difference between good and bad furniture. The question was, how?

He realized that it was unrealistic to hope that the public would acquire his knowledge of industrial manufacturing methods, modern material and design theory. But everyone had, at some point, held a hammer. Mari filled his studio with boards and started hammering. In contrast to furniture makers, who work with artisan joints, he was inspired by the simple construction principle that builders had used for workbenches and scaffolding for centuries: If you nail two boards together at the desired angle, you won't get any stability, but if you fix them with a diagonal board you have created a triangle – a construction that is practically impossible to budge. Using as few boards as possible, he hammered together a collection of furniture, without having to go back to the drawing board.

The designs were simple. They didn't require any slanted saw cuts or handicraft skills. He avoided giving exact measurements on his plans to encourage people to make their own adjustments and to increase their awareness of how the designs worked. *Autoprogettazione?* – a pamphlet with plans for 19 pieces of furniture – was distributed free to anyone who would pay for the postage. 'Open source' before the term was invented.

One reviewer in the newspaper *Paese Sera* enthusiastically summarized:

> 'With only one or two days' work, it's now possible to furnish a whole apartment with bed, chairs, table, wardrobe, bookshelf, desk and bench. The cost ends up at 40,000 lire per piece of furniture if you use planed timber. Half if you settle for rough timber ... Is it difficult? Not at all. You will neither have to glue nor join ... Is it naïve? Does he mean that everyone should start sawing boards and hammer together their own furniture? Mari is the first to admit that the initiative is utopian. But what is a designer to do when he – still unsuccessfully – has campaigned to replace contemporary trends with durable and cheap objects?'

Soon, thousands of letters and requests from newly converted amateur carpenters came through the letter box at Enzo Mari's studio. *Autoprogettazione?* seemed to have struck a chord with the zeitgeist and received more attention than anything else he had ever done.

But when Mari opened the envelopes he was filled with disappointment. Some letters came from people who had summer houses in the Rocky Mountains or chalets in the Alps and wanted to decorate them in a chic rustic style. Others came from naïve radicals who advocated for a return to a pre-industrial lifestyle. Most seemed to interpret the furniture as a part of an aesthetic trend, an – in Mari's eyes – kitschy romanticizing of untreated wood and pseudo-craftsmanship.

Merda pura.

Mari left *Autoprogettazione?* behind and moved on to new projects: steel furniture so thin that it appeared almost weightless; political art; hand-cast plastic vases. And he continued to argue.

In 2013 he closed the studio at Piazzale Baracca in Milan. In an interview with the design magazine *Klat*, the 81-year-old Mari summarized his deed: 'I have devoted my life to removing people's blinkers, but I've failed miserably.' The influential art critic Hans Ulrich Obrist had a more agreeable interpretation of the Italian's life's work: 'It's sad that Mari isn't better known than he is. But if he hadn't been so difficult and not refused to acknowledge the rules of the gallery and the market, he would have been regarded as one of the biggest [designers] today.'

The plans in *Autoprogettazione?* have, however, acquired a life of their own. The furniture can be seen in cafés, galleries and on 'do-it-yourself' sites on the internet. Mari's aesthetic legacy is clearly visible in the works of esteemed furniture designers such as Jasper Morrison, Kazuhide Takahama and Fredrik Paulsen. You could even say that the *Autoprogettazione?*

pieces have succeeded where Mari himself did not. In recent years, the ideas behind the furniture seem to have caught on. Young designers who have been captivated by the furniture's form have also embraced Mari's ideological pursuit for durability, function and simplicity.

To a certain extent the boom is probably due to the cyclical nature of trends, as pine and a self-build culture is popular again. But perhaps it's also just as much due to the furniture having an intrinsic quality. If you build one of Mari's tables, try placing it next to a table you have bought. The more expensive table, manufactured according to complex industrial models, will start to develop an identity crisis before your eyes.

Read this chapter before you start

You don't need a workshop, workbench or expensive machines to build the furniture in this book. Some basic tools and a flat surface on a floor or a sturdy dining table are sufficient. But it's important that you familiarize yourself with a few basic principles and techniques before you get going. If you follow them you have a good chance of succeeding in building furniture that is both durable, stylish and simple to construct.

Tools

ESSENTIAL ITEMS:

Hammer
Nails
Wood glue (or screwdriver and screws)
Saw (unless you get everything cut to size at
a hardware store or timber merchant)
Tape measure or folding ruler
A sharp pencil

USEFUL ITEMS:

Sandpaper
Sanding block
Carpenter's square
Drill
Wood oil, varnish, soap or paint
Pincers
Chisel

Wood

The designs in this book require planed timber that is 21mm thick. If your timber is slightly different adjust the measurements accordingly. For these pieces of furniture, I think pine will give the nicest result, and it's also one of the cheapest and most common types of wood. Pine is light in colour when freshly cut but will turn much more yellow once it has been oiled or exposed to light for a long time. Of course, you can also use other types of wood.

For tabletops and other large surfaces, you could, from a technical point of view, use plywood or chipboard, but the result will be more interesting if you join together several narrower boards.

When you're at the hardware store, it can be a good idea to do a quick survey and pick out the boards that look the best. Some people regard dark knots as blemishes, but I think they can be pretty. Avoid the most bent boards.

Joints

The plans and assembly instructions for the furniture don't include specific instructions for how to join the pieces of wood together. This is because there are several different methods. This next section outlines the most basic ones.

In addition to these, there are a range of more advanced techniques for making completely invisible joints. Since they require either advanced handicraft skills or expensive machinery, I haven't recommended using them for these furniture projects – the idea behind these designs is that they should openly showcase the method of their construction.

NAILS

There are many different kinds of nails. Wire nails are the most common variety and are suitable for this kind of woodwork. A wire nail has a large, flat head, which is good for outdoor furniture, since it stops water getting into the wood. If you don't like the visible heads you can use brad nails, which have a discreet conical head. If you're making outdoor furniture you should use galvanized nails, which won't rust.

If the wood is especially hard or just very dry, you can dip the nail into water, so that it goes into the boards more easily. This is why carpenters sometimes spit on the nails.

When nailing, you should grip the hammer as far down on the handle as possible to make use of its full force. Every joint needs two nails. Avoid driving them in along the same grain line. This is because the end grain and edges will easily split when you drive in the

nails, especially if the timber is thin. To further reduce the risk of splits, you can dull the point of the nail with a blow from the hammer.

It's a good idea to use a ruler to position the nail heads symmetrically and in a line. Where possible, you should drive in the nails at an angle and overlapping to make the joint more secure. If the nail bends, pull it out and drive a new one into the same hole but from a different direction. If you're left with an ugly mark on the wood after pulling out the nail, you can dab the surface with warm water. This will cause the fibres to rise. When the wood has dried, sand the area down with sandpaper.

To get the best hold possible, at least two-thirds of the length of the nail should penetrate into the backing board. Most boards in this book are 21mm thick. When you join one of those you should therefore, as a rule, use a nail that is at least 60mm long. In many of the constructions, the material that you join onto has the same dimensions, which means that a 60mm-long nail would protrude on the other side. In this case you'll have to use a 40mm-long nail, and reinforce the joint with wood glue applied to the surface of the boards.

And since you've already got the glue out, I recommend that you use it for all nailed joints. You don't want to risk your homemade chair collapsing. A secure alternative, if you don't mind a very crude appearance, is to drive the long nail all the way through and fold it over properly against the surface in the direction of the grain on the other side – but you can't tell my old teacher at the cabinet-making school in Rødovre outside Copenhagen that I said that.

WOOD GLUE

As mentioned, if you assemble the furniture with nails I recommend reinforcing the joints with glue. If the furniture is intended for outdoor use, choose a wood glue that is resistant to frost and damp.

Squeeze out a few lines of glue over both surfaces – it should be just the right amount so that a small white line of glue is squeezed out from between the pieces of wood when they are pressed together. If you want you can use a brush to apply thin, even layers. Place the timber into the required position and fix with nails or screws. Make sure that the boards are properly pressed together and leave the joint to dry. Use a damp cloth to remove any visible glue. If you don't, you can leave it to dry and then scrape the glue off with a knife or a chisel. Sand off any remaining traces of the glue.

SCREWS

In terms of strength, self-drilling screws are superior to nails and with an electric screwdriver it's easier to get more precision in the joints. However, the screw heads can give a more industrial appearance that might not suit all furniture.

To ensure that the wood doesn't split when you screw, you can pre-drill the holes. The drill hole should in that case be slightly shorter and narrower than the screw. If you don't pre-drill you should, just as when you use nails, avoid placing several screws along the same line of wood grain. Another trick to avoid splits is to not screw in the whole screw at once. Instead, screw it in 10–22mm, pull it back halfway, then drive it in a further 10–20mm and continue like this until the screw head is level with the surface.

It's a good idea to measure out with a ruler so that you can place the screws in a straight line, with even gaps between them. Use a wood screw with a flat head that doesn't require pre-drilling. The screw should be around double the length of the thickness of the timber that you are joining (without the point protruding at the back). As almost all boards in this book are 21mm thick, you should, as a rule, use 40mm long screws.

You can hide the screws completely with wood plugs. The result will be more elegant but it's a bit more fiddly and goes against Mari's principles for these particular furniture pieces. If you still want to attach wood plugs, you drill with a twist drill in the diameter of the screw head, the same depth as the thickness of the plug. Pre-drill with a thinner drill for the screw, drive the screw in all the way and glue the plug into the hole. Then use a chisel and sandpaper to even out the surface.

ASSEMBLING BOARDS IN A ROW

When you assemble several boards in a row, to make a tabletop for example, place them so that the direction of the end grain's growth rings alternates. Wood is a living material which will move when the moisture content in the wood and in the air changes. By placing the heart side facing alternate ways, the tensions in the wood will pull in different directions which will lower the chance of the tabletop bulging – particularly if it has been glued.

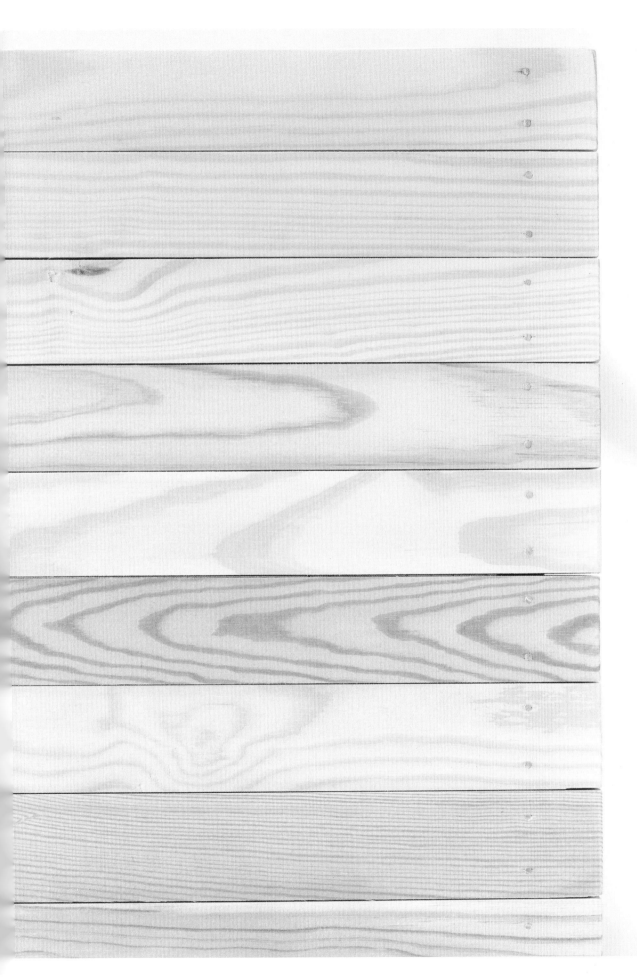

Saw

If you are just building a singular piece of furniture, it's easiest to take the cutting list to the store when you buy timber and get it sawn to size. Then the measurements will be correct, and the cuts will be nice and straight. Take the surplus timber home with you to use for spares, in case something goes wrong.

If you want to cut the timber yourself, you can use pretty much any wood saw as long as you measure carefully. The furniture in the book only requires standard straight cuts. If you only have a standard handsaw, that will do the job, although the cuts won't be as nice as they would be using, for example, a backsaw or a Japanese saw. Regardless of which type of saw you're using, the teeth will need to be sharp. Hold the saw straight and run it back and forth without applying too much pressure. It's a good idea to use a mitre box, which will make cutting straight easier.

Using a square can also help to get a straight pencil line to saw along.

Sandpaper

Sandpaper, or abrasive paper, comes in different grit sizes, which is specified on the back. The higher the number, the finer the grain. Since the plans in this book use planed timber, you actually only need to sand the saw cuts, the edges and the corners. For this, a fairly fine sandpaper is enough, with a grit size of between 180 and 320. I usually sand the timber quickly after I have cut it to size with a sanding block made from cork. Then I go over the assembled furniture a bit more carefully with sandpaper to bevel edges and corners. For this, it's good to work without a block so that the paper is moulded to your fingers and follows the wood. Don't just sand the visible parts, but also smooth over the edges you will hold when lifting the piece of furniture. Remember to always sand in the direction of the grain.

Surface treatment

If the furniture is made for indoor use you don't have to treat it and it will develop an organic patina over time. It will, however, also be more susceptible to stains and wear.

   If you want to paint, oil or varnish the furniture, you will get the best results if you do this before assembling the parts. If you are using an opaque paint the nail or screw heads will stand out more. If you don't want them to be visible, you can just dab them with a little paint once assembled.

Plans

Before you start a project, I recommend that you study its plan carefully. This contains basically all the information that you will need.

On the whole, the step-by-step assembly instructions can be regarded as suggestions for the order in which to assemble the different parts. Seasoned home carpenters might not need the assembly instructions at all, but can instead work from just the cutting lists and the plans.

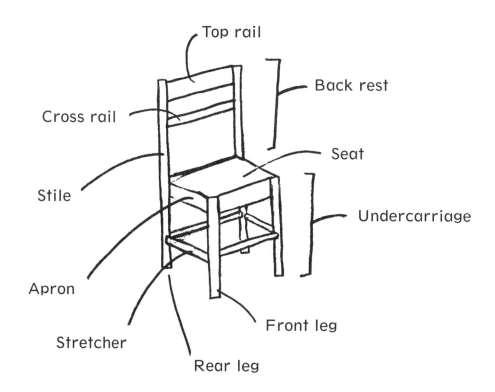

The anatomy of a chair – if you memorize the names of the different parts of seating furniture, it will be easier to follow the descriptions (see page 47).

Designing your own furniture

One of my main hopes with this book is that it will inspire inexperienced carpenters to build their own furniture. However, you don't have to follow the plans slavishly. On the contrary, I call on you to regard the plans as suggestions rather than a definitive guide.
All the furniture in the book is constructed by drawing on a few common principles. If you follow them, you can easily design your own pieces similar to those in this book:

› Only use straight saw cuts.
› Join the boards in as simple a way as possible. A good rule of thumb is that anyone looking at the piece of furniture should understand how it is assembled. It's better to assemble the boards overlapping, on top, or on the outside of each other.
› Avoid adding features that aren't necessary for function, stability or comfort.
› Let the function steer the design.

In addition to these principles, there are a few measurements that it is good to be aware of to make sure the furniture is made to standard scale:

Chair seat height, front: 400–450mm
Chair seat height, rear: 1–50mm lower than the front height
Seat angle (between seat and back rest): 93–110 degrees
Chair seat depth: 370–460mm
Chair seat width: at least 360mm

Armrest height: approximately 200mm higher than the front of the seat

Width between armrests: at least 430mm

Table height: 300mm higher than the seat, that is 700–750mm

Tabletop: every person needs approximately 600mm of width to not feel squeezed in, and at least 350mm of depth to be able to fit a plate, cutlery and a glass. A rectangular table for four people should therefore be at least 1200mm (600 + 600) long and 700mm (350 + 350) deep

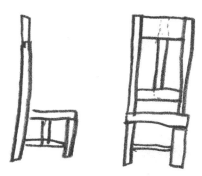

REMEMBER!

1. Study plans and images carefully. They will often give more guidance than the step-by-step instructions.
2. The instructions should primarily be regarded as suggestions for the order in which to carry out the different steps.
3. To 'join' means that you either use glue and nails, or screws. All nailed joints will need at least two nails.
4. A diagram with the names of the different parts of seating furniture can be found on page 44.

Furniture

Sheep chair

This is a slightly altered version of the most iconic
chair in Enzo Mari's book *Autoprogettazione?* I think
it resembles a ewe with its slightly bulky body and thin
legs. It's a good piece to start with as it's so easy to
build and the construction is ingenious in its simplicity.
The apron is so wide that the chair doesn't require
a stabilizing stretcher. Despite its weight and rustic
appearance, it's remarkably comfortable.

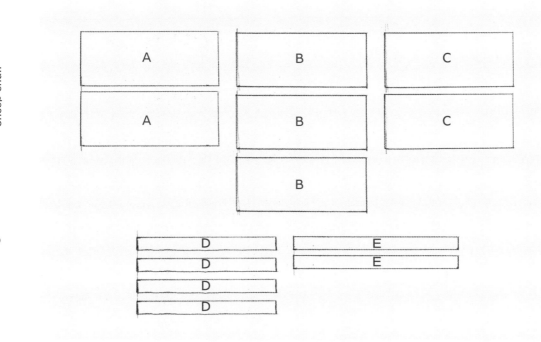

Piece	Dimension	Length	Quantity
A	195 × 21mm	520mm	2
B	195 × 21mm	475mm	3
C	195 × 21mm	470mm	2
D	43 × 21mm	440mm	4
E	43 × 21mm	610mm	2

1. Start by assembling the sides: attach the legs (D) to the apron's sides (C).

2. Attach the stiles (E) onto the sides of the apron (C). To get a good angle on the back rest, the stiles should sit against the rear legs at the top, but have a 35mm gap between them at the bottom.

3. Nail or screw the sides to the front and rear of the apron (B). To give the seat a good angle, the rear apron should be joined 21mm below the edge of C and the back legs.

4. Next, put the seat pieces (A) in place and join.

5. Assemble the back rest by nailing or screwing the top rail (B) onto the stiles (E).

Side view

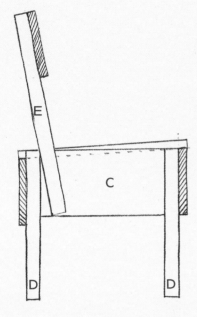

Front view

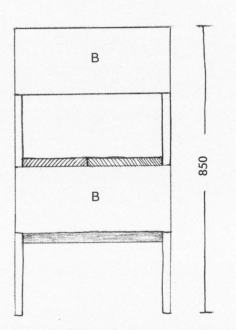

850

Top view

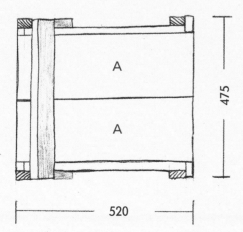

475

520

Tilting Shaker chair

The Shaker movement was in its heyday in the 19th century and was mostly renowned for two things: its ecstatic dancing during worship and its handicrafts.

You could say that the beliefs and philosophy of the movement took expression in design. Function directed the form and details that were purely decorative were banned. In return, every cut, every joint and surface treatment was to be made with as much care as possible. This way, the material and the construction were decoration enough.

Shaker chairs often had a woven seat and ladder back rest, and the top rail could be hung on one of the pegs that were fixed to the walls of the movement's communal dwellings. This way, they didn't only free up floor space, the hanging chairs also doubled as decorative objects.

One problem for everyone who designs chairs is how to get a comfortable tilt on the seat and the back. Some time ago, I saw a picture of an old Shaker chair, where the carpenter had solved the ergonomic challenge by letting the whole chair tilt.

Here I have used that concept and tried to combine the Shaker chair's characteristics with Enzo Mari's simple construction principles.

1. Start with the back rest: firstly, join the bottom D-piece 43mm from the bottom of both stiles (G). Continue with the rest of the D-pieces, working from the bottom up. The gap in between them should be 148.5mm, top edge to top edge.

2. Assemble one of the front legs (B) with one of the stretchers (A), so that the stretcher sits 30mm away from the bottom edges of the legs. You can use a square to make sure you have a right angle. Then repeat with the other front leg and the other stretcher – but mirrored.

3. Join the two side pieces (C) of the apron to the top edge of the front legs. Make sure you have a right angle.

4. Join the two front legs together by joining the front part (E) of the apron at the interior right angle made at the join between B and C.

5. Assemble the back together with the front part. Make sure that the bottom stretcher protrudes 70mm behind the rear leg.

6. Put the parts of the seat (F) in place and join. Remember to alternate the direction of the end grain's growth rings (see page 36).

Piece	Dimension	Length	Quantity
A	43 × 21mm	500mm	2
B	43 × 21mm	460mm	2
C	43 × 21mm	430mm	2
D	43 × 21mm	430mm	7
E	43 × 21mm	430mm	1
F	43 × 21mm	430mm	9
G	43 × 21mm	998mm	2

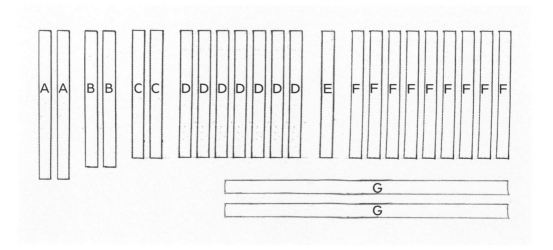

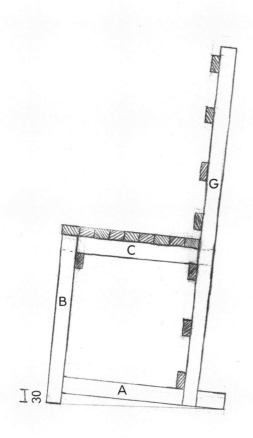

Side view

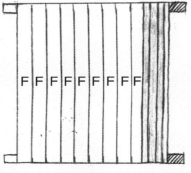

Top view

430

148.5
148.5
148.5
148.5
148.5
148.5
148.5

30

A
B
C
G
D
D
D
D
E
D
D
D
F F F F F F F F F

Front view

Pinnstol/Windsor chair

In the middle of the 19th century, a noblewoman from Småland in southern Sweden caught sight of an American chair with turned spindles that were slotted into the seat. She liked it so much that she commissioned a carpenter in Svenarum to build some similar chairs using local birch wood.

The chairs were so admired that the carpenter started to specialize in these Windsor chairs, or Pinnstolar, as the local variation became known. Other carpenters soon followed in his footsteps and during the following years, several Pinnstol factories opened in Småland. Soon the Pinnstol became one of the most common pieces of furniture in the country.

Sweden is still full of Pinnstolar. They can be found in run-down cabins and damp community centres, in star-studded restaurants and in designer stores. It is an ingenious piece of furniture in many ways as it's comfortable and doesn't use a lot of materials. It lacks all unnecessary finery and can be unassumingly beautiful. It's a piece of furniture for the people, with roots in both old folk craft and industrial production. The chair of chairs.

I wanted to explore whether it was possible to produce a Pinnstol or Windsor chair that was as simple in its construction as a mass-produced factory chair, but still had the personality of a handmade chair – without using either industrial tools or cabinet-maker techniques. All the boards are 430mm long, apart from the rear legs which are exactly double the length.

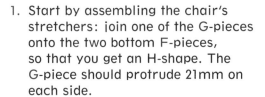

1. Start by assembling the chair's stretchers: join one of the G-pieces onto the two bottom F-pieces, so that you get an H-shape. The G-piece should protrude 21mm on each side.

2. Join the same F-pieces to the insides of the legs (A and C), 150mm from the ground.

3. Assemble the apron. To give the seat a suitable tilt, the two remaining F-pieces should be joined to the rear legs (A) 370mm up from the floor. Their top edges should line up with the top edge of the rear of the front legs – in this way they will protrude slightly above the legs at the front. Then join the two remaining G-pieces to the legs so that they sit against the bottom edge of the F-pieces.

4. Put the seat pieces (B) in place. Join to F.

5. Time to assemble the back rest's top rail (E) onto the back of the stiles (A). The upper edge of the back rest should sit 430mm above the bottom of the seat. Use one of the back's spindles (D) as a way of measuring.

6. When you join the spindles (D) to the top rail and the seat, the back rest will sit at a comfortable angle. The distance between them should be 43mm – so you can use the spindles for measuring. It's a good idea to lay the chair down so that it is supported by the floor when you join the spindles, especially if you are using a hammer.

Side view

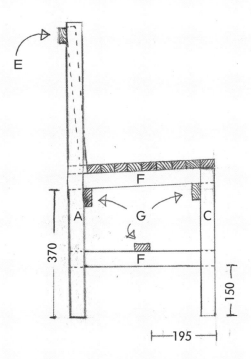

E

F

A   G   C

370

F

150

195

Front view

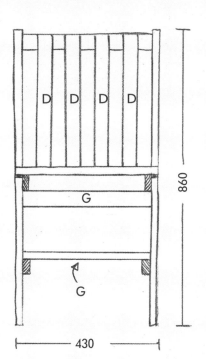

D D D D

G

G

860

430

Top view

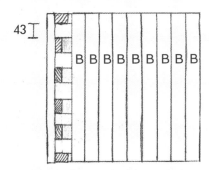

43

B B B B B B B B B

Piece	Dimension	Length	Quantity
A	21 × 43mm	860mm	2
B	21 × 43mm	430mm	9
C	21 × 43mm	430mm	2
D	21 × 43mm	430mm	4
E	21 × 43mm	430mm	1
F	21 × 43mm	430mm	4
G	21 × 43mm	430mm	3

Garden chair

This is one of Enzo Mari's *Autoprogettazione?* chairs that I have adapted for outdoor use. The gaps between the slats of the seat make it easy to carry and will drain off any rainwater. In contrast to most of the other pieces of furniture in this book, it has almost no right angles. As a result, it demands a little bit more from the person who holds the tools.

The plan contains all the information you need to build a chair that is almost identical to the one in the picture dependent on the angles you use. It will be easier for you if, you draw on your own instincts to make sure the angles are suitable, rather than following the plan to the letter.

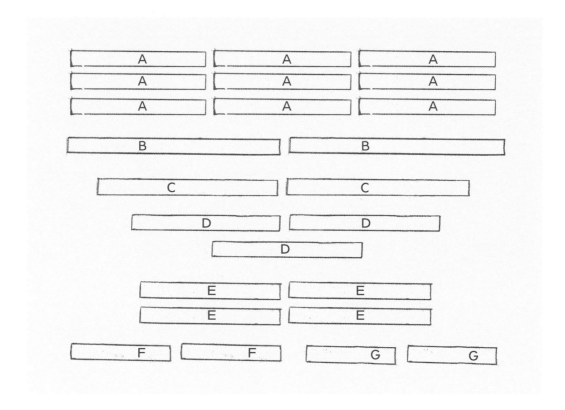

1. Lay the parts for one side of the chair out onto your work surface. Arrange them in the correct formation according to the plan, with the rear leg (C) at the bottom. Lay out the stretcher (F) and apron (E) at the next level and front leg (E) and stile (B) at the top. You can place another board along the bottom edge to see how the rear and front legs will stand on the floor. It's important that you get the right tilt on the seat and back rest. Assemble!

2. Use the finished side as a template when you lay out the parts for the other side, mirroring the first, and assemble them.

3. Join both sides by fixing the A-pieces to the rear legs so that they support the angles under F and E respectively.

4. Join the front stretcher (D) to both front legs so that it supports F.

5. Stand behind the chair and measure diagonally between the corners in the rectangle that is formed between the rear legs (C) and the two A-pieces. Adjust so that the distances between the corners are equal. Fix into place with the G-pieces.

6. Lay the chair down and join the top rails (D) to the stiles. The distance between them should be 43mm. Use one of the remaining pieces for measuring.

7. Put the pieces for the seat (A) in position, evenly spaced. Fix into place.

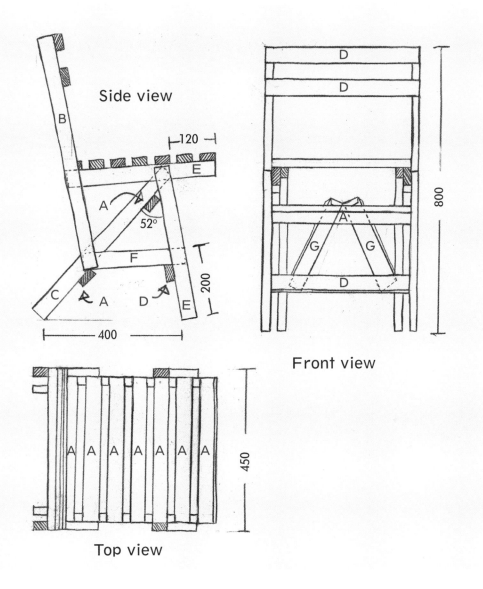

Side view

Front view

Top view

Piece	Dimension	Length	Quantity
A	43 × 21mm	408mm	9
B	43 × 21mm	650mm	2
C	43 × 21mm	550mm	2
D	43 × 21mm	450mm	3
E	43 × 21mm	430mm	4
F	43 × 21mm	300mm	2
G	43 × 21mm	270mm	2

Arts and Crafts chair

During the Industrial Revolution many handicraft trades were replaced by machines. The new factories spewed out goods that were certainly cheaper and easier to produce, but they were not as high quality. Their shortcomings were in turn compensated for by machine-produced ornament and decoration.

In the middle of the 19th century, a group of artists and craftspeople gathered in protest to this and this became the Arts & Crafts movement. They advocated for a pronounced anti-industrial aesthetic, where the furniture should show clear marks of the carpenters' hands. Many objects were even left a bit unfinished to demonstrate their organically personal character.

This chair is inspired by the Arts and Crafts movements' typical armchairs – with a high back rest, right angles and slender legs and armrests. You can regard it as the fruit of an experiment: what happens if you borrow the design ethos from the anti-industrial and handicrafts-loving Arts and Crafts movement, but use factory-planed timber and construct a chair according to simplified mass-production principles so that any old wonky-hammering person can assemble the chair?

The result is neither handicraft piece nor industrial product, but carries clear marks of the carpenter's touch.

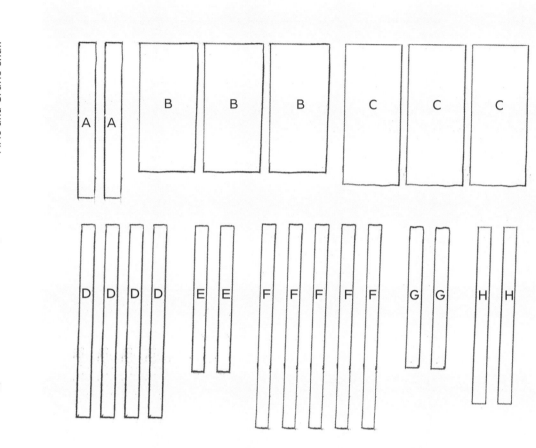

Piece	Dimension	Length	Quantity
A	43 × 21mm	415mm	2
B	195 × 21mm	420mm	3
C	195 × 21mm	460mm	3
D	43 × 21mm	640mm	4
E	43 × 21mm	481mm	2
F	43 × 21mm	671mm	5
G	43 × 21mm	460mm	2
H	43 × 21mm	585mm	2

Side view

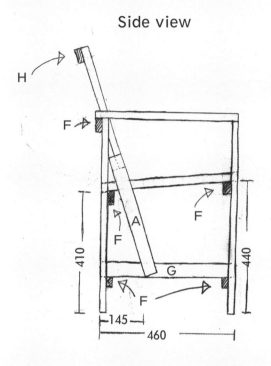

Front view

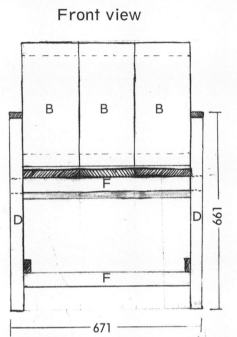

Top view

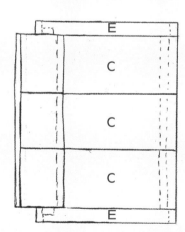

1. Start with one of the sides: join the armrest (E) to the top of the legs (D) so that it protrudes 21mm at the back. Join the stretcher (G) to the inside of the legs (D), 125mm from the bottom.

2. Use the finished side as a template and follow the instructions in step 1 to assemble the other side the same way, but mirrored.

3. Join the two sides using the five F-pieces according to the plan: the bottom ones should sit just under the stretcher (G); the top one should sit under the parts of the armrests (E) that protrude over the rear legs. Note that the middle ones should sit at different heights – the top edge of the front F-piece should sit 440mm from the bottom of the front legs, the rear top edge 410mm from the bottom of the rear legs.

4. Assemble the seat. Put the C-pieces in place on top of the apron (F), so that it tilts backwards slightly. Fix into place.

5. Time to give some stability to the chair! Carefully measure diagonally from corner to corner in the rectangles that have formed on each side between G, D and E. Make sure that the distances are equal. Then fix the construction with the struts (A) according to the plan: join the A-struts to G, 145mm away from the rear edges of G, so that their bottom corners align with the bottom of G when their top sides rest against the rear legs (D). Then join the struts to the sides of the seat (C).

6. Assemble the back rest: lay out the parts for the back rest (B) onto the work surface. Join them together with an H-piece at the top edge and one at the bottom.

7. Lay the chair down on one side. Insert the back rest between the armrests and position it so that the top side of the back rest's lower H-piece aligns with the tilting struts' (A) top side while the back rest sits against the top F-piece. Secure the back rest into place by joining A to H and B, then join the back rest pieces to the top F-piece.

Ski chair

This chair is also an adaptation of one of Enzo Mari's pieces of furniture. The design is quite special and a bit contradictory. While it looks heavy, sturdy and angular, the over-dimensioned gaps means that you can see straight through it. The back rest's protruding boards bring to mind three skis sticking out from a chairlift.

1. Start by assembling the two rear legs (D) by joining the two H-pieces across the top of one of their thin sides. The lower piece should sit 250mm from the bottom. The upper, 40mm from the top.

2. Measure diagonally between the corners of the legs and adjust until the distances are equal. Fix into place with G.

3. Assemble one of the sides together by joining one of the front legs (F) to the outside of the apron (E) so that it has a very slight backwards tilt.

4. Use the finished side as a template and then assemble the other side mirrored, but with the same angle.

5. Assemble the sides together by joining the rear seat board (A).

It should protrude 21mm from the apron (E) on both sides.

6. Join the front legs to the outside of the assembled rear legs so that the rear legs' upper corners are in contact with the apron. The angle will be correct when F is straight and the rear legs' lower corners rest on the ground.

7. Assemble the back rest's two B-pieces by joining them to the lower H-piece and the seat's assembled A-board. The back rest should stop about 850mm from the floor. When done, attach E and D to the two B-pieces

8. Join C centred between the two B-boards.

9. Assemble the remaining three boards (A) for the seat, spaced out evenly.

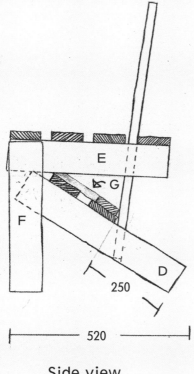

850

520

250

E

G

F

D

Side view

B   C   B

H

H

450

Front view

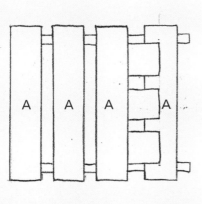

A   A   A   A

Top view

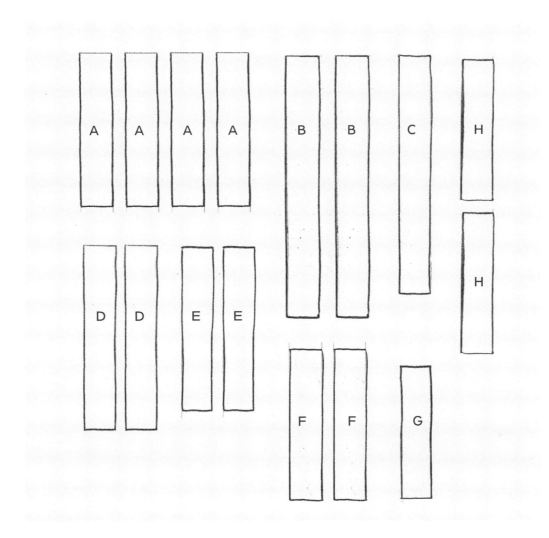

Piece	Dimension	Length	Quantity
A	95 × 21mm	450mm	4
B	95 × 21mm	760mm	2
C	95 × 21mm	700mm	1
D	95 × 21mm	540mm	2
E	95 × 21mm	480mm	2
F	95 × 21mm	440mm	2
G	95 × 21mm	385mm	1
H	95 × 21mm	408mm	2

Mirror stool

The stool is the mother of chairs and one of the first pieces of furniture constructed by humans. It was also the first piece of furniture that all the students got to design and build when I did a course in cabinet-making in Denmark.

The stool is also a good example of why you shouldn't complicate things unless you have no choice. Since it's often so simple in its design, it can have all sorts of uses. It can be used as a seat, table, extra surface or as a step when you want to reach the top kitchen shelf.

This model draws inspiration from two sources: first, the sturdy pine chair made up of two parts that the architect Charlotte Perriand designed for a ski resort in the Savoie in France in the sixties; second, a stool with a lateral bar that makes it possible to carry upside down as a basket, that the design rector Max Bill designed for his students at the German Ulm School of Design in 1955 and which became the school's primary piece of furniture.

To simplify the assembly and minimize the number of parts, I have off-centred the two halves. This way you can join the wide lateral stretcher to the legs from two sides. At the same time, the off-centring gives the furniture a sense of double exposure – as if one half is the other's shadow or reflection.

Piece	Dimension	Length	Quantity
A	143 × 21mm	420mm	2
B	143 × 21mm	420mm	2
C	143 × 21mm	441mm	2
D	143 × 21mm	505mm	1

1. Start by assembling one of the stool's two halves: join the seat (A) to the top side of the shorter leg (B) and to the side of the longer leg (C) so that you get the shape of an upside-down U.

2. Do the same with the remaining A-, B- and C-pieces to build the other half of the stool.

3. Lay one half down onto your work surface. Make sure that the corners have right angles. Then fix into place by joining the stretcher (D) to both legs, 143mm from the bottom. D should protrude 21mm from the long leg (C). It should protrude double the amount from the short leg.

4. Place the stool half on the floor to check that it stands straight. If not, you'll have to go back to step 3 and make sure that all angles are true.

5. Place the remaining half in a mirrored position against the finished half so that each side has one long (C) and one short (B) leg. The shorter legs should be placed 21mm further in than the long legs on both sides.

6. Make sure that all the corners have right angles. Screw or nail through the stretcher (D) into the legs on the unassembled half.

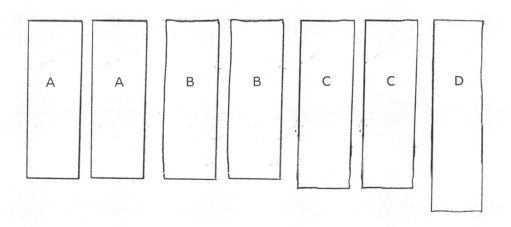

Side view

Front view

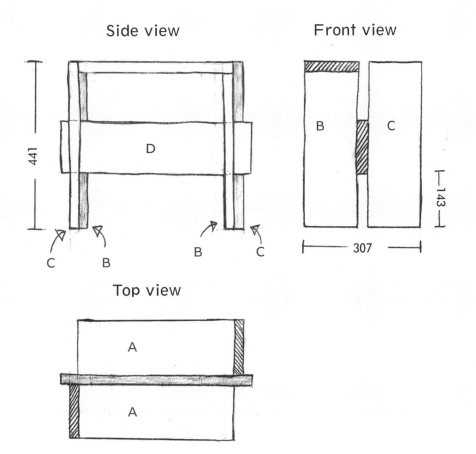

Top view

Stackable
stool

This construction is based on the same principles as the Sheep chair (page 51). But since the seat is straight and the bottom edge of the apron sits at the same height on all sides, you can stack several on top of each other.

The idea is that you will be able to have a stack of stools in a corner to put out around the table when you have extra guests.

Piece	Dimension	Length	Quantity
A	95 × 21mm	340mm	4
B	95 × 21mm	385mm	3
C	95 × 21mm	370mm	4
D	43 × 21mm	440mm	4

1. Assemble the front and the back: join the legs (D) along the edge of the apron's front and back sides (A).

2. Join the sides (C) to the outsides of the finished front and back sides.

3. Join the three boards for the seat (B) so they rest on the C-boards in between the A-sides.

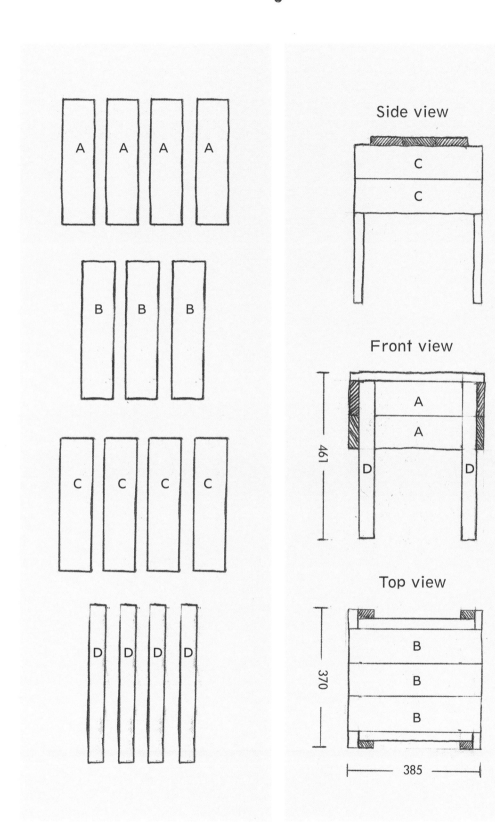

Side view

C
C

Front view

A
A

D   D

461

Top view

B
B
B

370

385

Beer table

The inspiration for this coffee table is a beer crate.

I lived in Copenhagen for a few years where many antique dealers sold old, wooden beer crates from Carlsberg. The cuboid design and the dimensions made them very versatile and they worked just as well as stools, boxes, shelves and coffee tables.

This piece of furniture is primarily designed to be used as a smaller coffee table, but it is of course suitable to be used for whatever you want. It is more cube-shaped than a beer crate and has three open sides instead of one.

A piece of furniture can't be much simpler than this: the two sides and the tabletop are joined together by two laths and a lateral stretcher at the bottom gives stability to the construction whilst also working as a shelf.

Front view

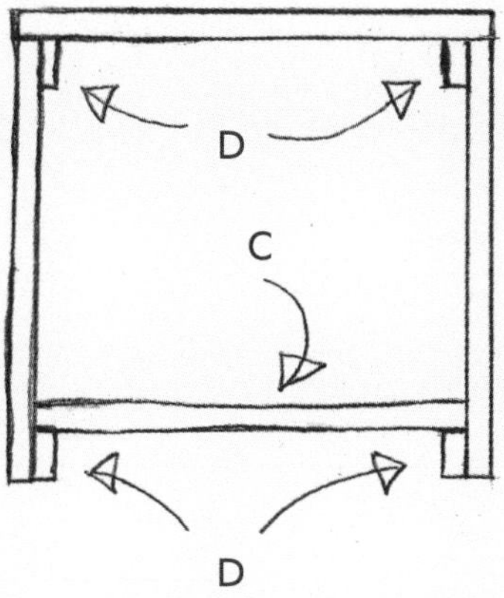

Top view

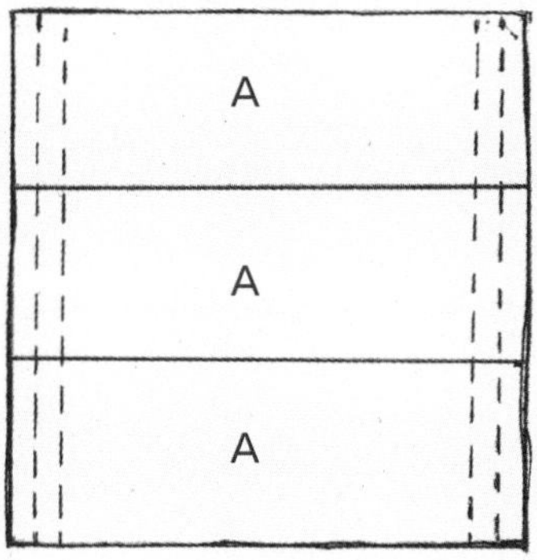

Side view

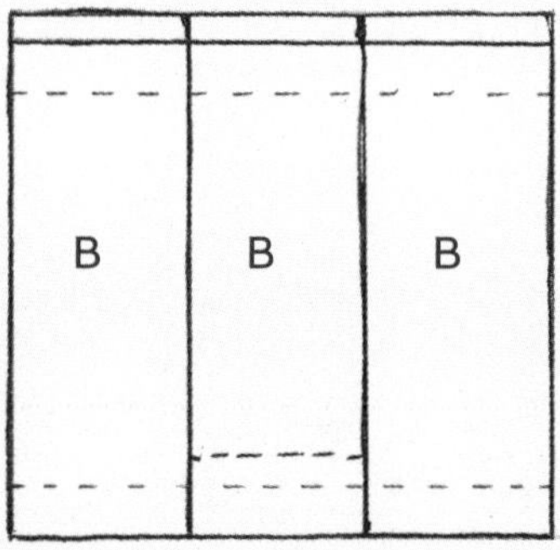

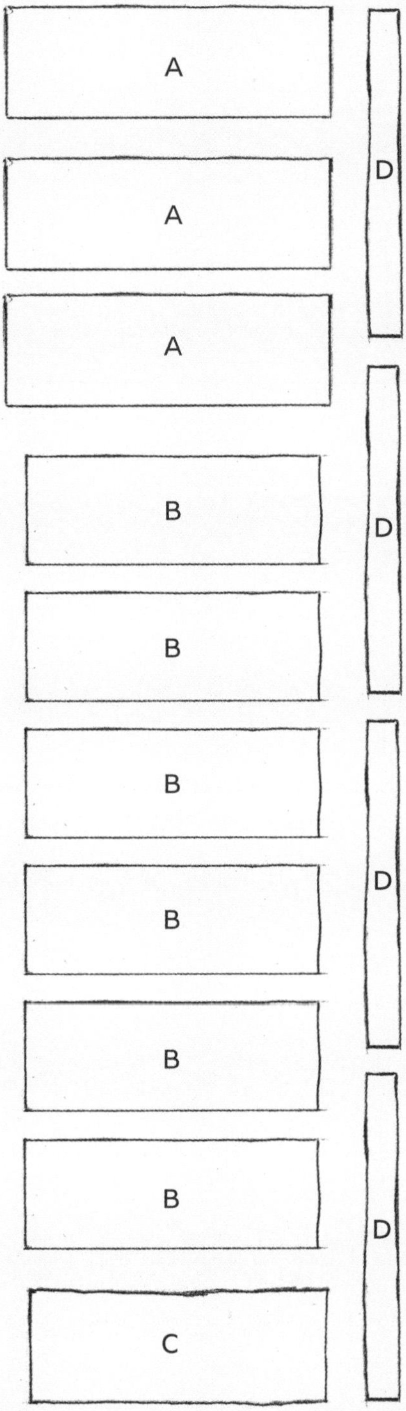

Piece	Dimension	Length	Quantity
A	21 × 143mm	430mm	3
B	21 × 143mm	380mm	6
C	21 × 143mm	388mm	1
D	21 × 43mm	429mm	4

1. Start with one of the sides: assemble the B-pieces with the help of a lath (D), one at the bottom and one at the top. Make sure that the top and bottom edges are completely level.

2. Repeat for the remaining B and D-pieces to build the other side.

3. Stand the sides up and put the boards for the seat (A) in place. Join them to D, so that the seat is aligned with the sides.

4. Lay the stretcher (C) in place on top of the bottom D-pieces, inside the side's middle B-pieces. Fix into position.

Kitchen bench

This is a longer version of the Sheep chair (page 51) but here we also make use of the deep apron for storage by building in a base, with the seat doubling up as a removable lid. This way you can hide away things you need but don't want displayed.

Note that the lid (A) and the base (B) don't have a standard width. You will therefore need to saw a piece to the correct measurement – or ask the staff at your hardware store to do so.

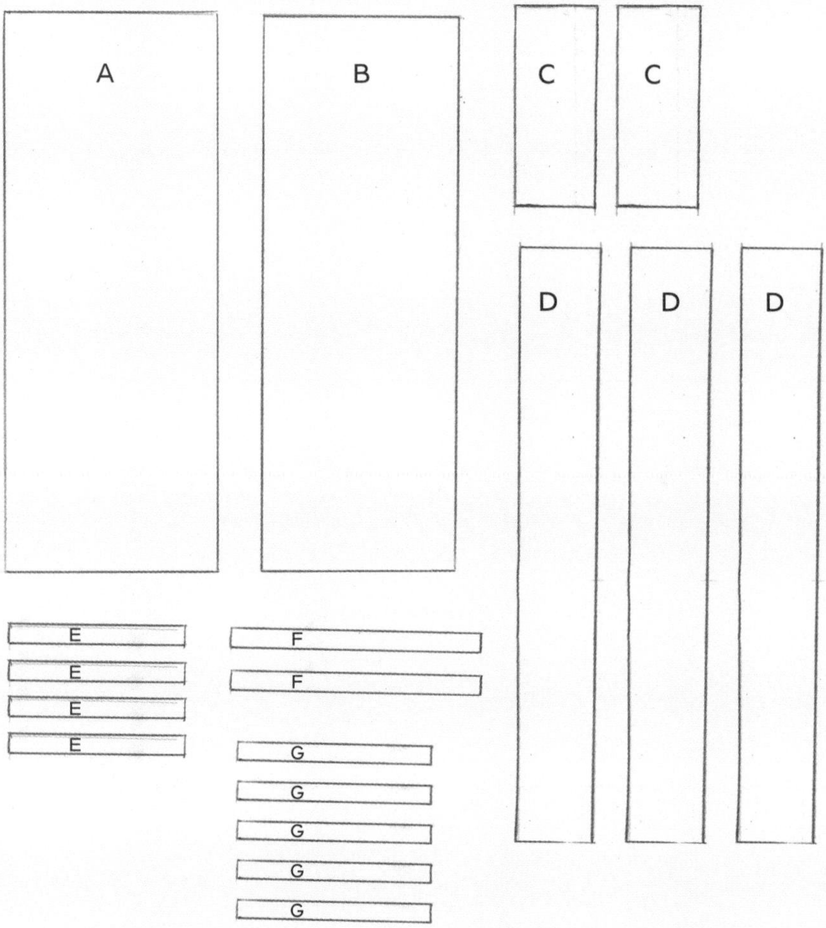

Piece	Dimension	Length	Quantity
A	520 × 21mm	1316mm	1
B	470 × 21mm	1316mm	1
C	195 × 21mm	470mm	2
D	195 × 21mm	1400mm	3
E	43 × 21mm	440mm	4
F	43 × 21mm	610mm	2
G	43 × 21mm	467mm	5

F

Side view

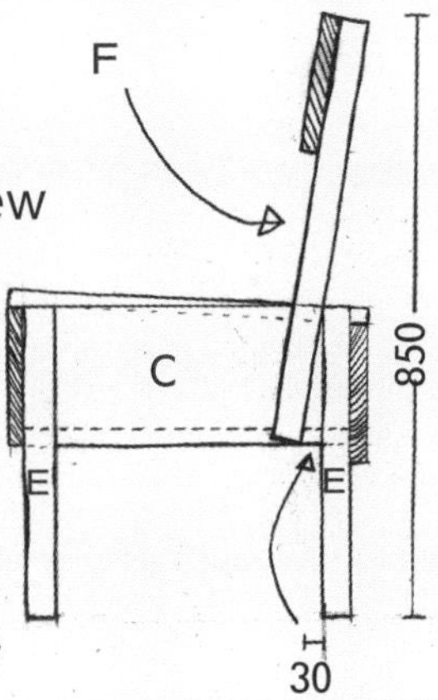

C

850

E   E

Front view

30

D

850

D

461

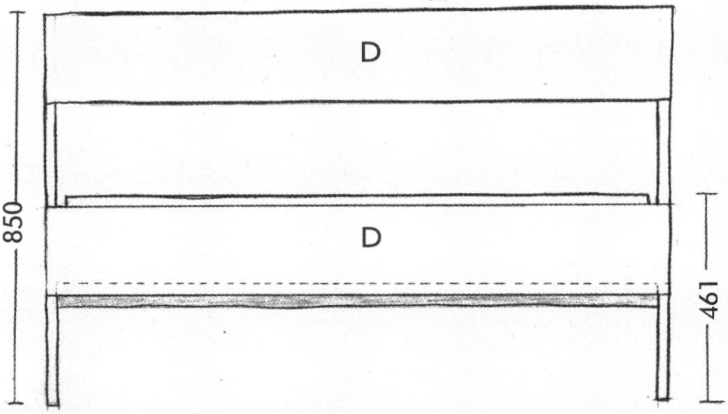

Top view without lid and back rest

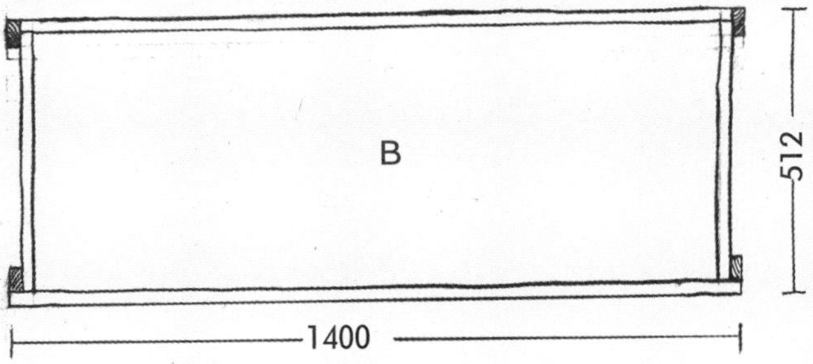

B

512

1400

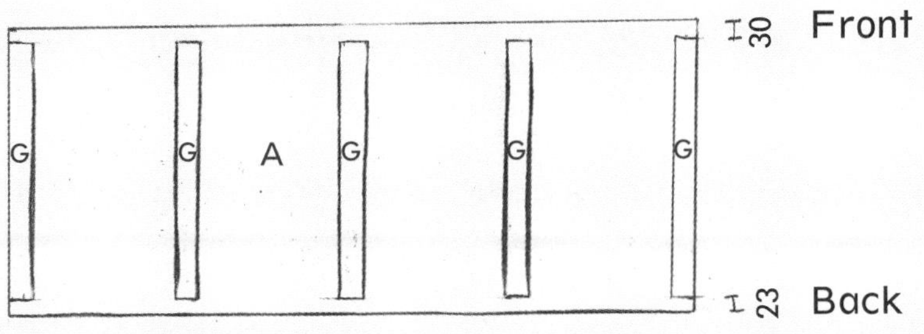

30 Front

G   G   A   G   G   G

23 Back

Lid, underside

1. Start by assembling the sides: join the legs (E) to the sides (C) of the apron.

2. Nail or screw the sides together with the apron's front and back (D). To give the seat a good tilt, the back apron should be joined 21mm under the edge.

3. Insert the bottom sheet (B) into the bench and join it so that it aligns with the bottom edges of the front and the sides.

4. Join the stiles (F) to the sides (C) of the apron. To get a good tilt on the back rest, the stiles should sit against the rear legs at the top, but 30mm away at the bottom. Secure them properly with three nails or screws in each so that the back rest is secure.

5. Carefully lay the bench down on its back and assemble the back rest (D).

6. Join the G-laths to the bottom of the lid according to the plan.

7. Put the lid in position. Mind your fingers!

Park bench

This is a simple and comfortable bench that is suitable for outdoor use. The design is Enzo Mari's. I have only adjusted it a little to make it possible to make with planed timber from a store.

You can of course also use it indoors together with a table, but I think the humble design with the two back boards brings to mind the type of bench that usually stands solitary underneath a gnarled oak in a park or on a jetty by the sea.

1. Start with one of the sides: use the front leg (G) as the starting point, which should stand straight. Join the apron (also G) so that it protrudes 60mm in the front of the leg, with a slight backwards tilt.

2. Assemble the rear leg (H). You will find the right angle when one of H's upper corners sits level with G's upper rear corner (according to the plan) and one of H's lower corners stands on the ground at the same time as the front leg (G) stands straight. Fix the angles by joining the stretcher (F). It should be joined 85mm from the ground on the front leg (measure at the front edge) and have about the same tilt as the apron.

3. Nail or screw the stile (D) into place. It should sit 405mm in from the top of the apron (G) to make sure that the seat ends up in the right place. You will have to trust your own judgement when you decide on the tilt, but you should get a good result if you let D's bottom corner sit edge to edge with the stretcher's (F) bottom edge – as on the plan.

4. Time for the second side. Lay the pieces out on top of the finished side and use it as a template. Remember that they should be mirrored, and the legs (G) and (H) should sit the furthest out on both sides (see page 107).

5. Assemble the middle support (I, G, J, E). Use one of the sides as a template to make sure you place G and E at the right angle. Next, place one of the shorter boards on top of the side template's stretcher (F) where the B-piece should sit. Then join the J-piece to the middle support (E) so that the piece that sits on top of F just fits in underneath it. Fix into place with the I-piece according to the plan. This sounds more complicated than it is. The point is that J and F have to be in the right place in relation to each other so that the B-board can then join together the sides and the middle support without it becoming wonky.

6. Thread the sides and the middle support onto the B-board. Join the sides at the outside edges and the middle support at the centre.

7. Join the back rests (A) to the stiles (D and E).

8. Measure diagonally between the sides' edges and adjust the bench sideways until the distances between the corners are equal. Then fix into place with the C-pieces.

9. Put the seat (A) in place. The front board should have an overhang of 15mm. The back board should sit against the stiles. Join the other two so that the gaps are even.

Piece	Dimension	Length	Quantity
A	95 × 21mm	1600mm	6
B	95 × 21mm	1200mm	1
C	95 × 21mm	810mm	2
D	95 × 21mm	750mm	2
E	95 × 21mm	690mm	1
F	95 × 21mm	450mm	2
G	95 × 21mm	440mm	5
H	95 × 21mm	420mm	2
I	95 × 21mm	330mm	1
J	95 × 21mm	300mm	1

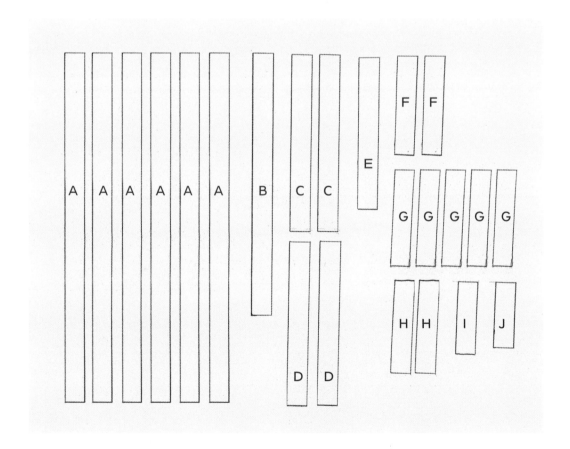

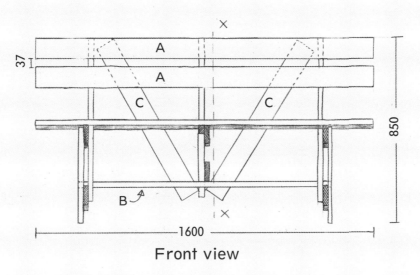

Front view

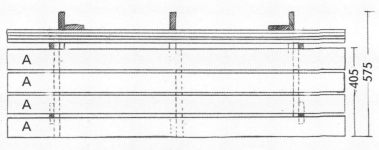

Top view

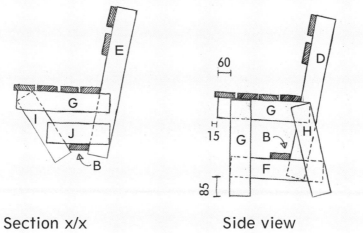

Section x/x   Side view

Sofa

This is an asymmetrical sofa with a back rest so high it can almost work as a room divider.

After seeing a picture of the author P. O. Enquist, snuggled up with his standard Schnauzer among sheepskins on a short sofa, I got the idea to build some kind of library furniture. A sofa where you could lie back, supported by cushions with your head in the corner and read a book, shielded away from everything that happens behind you. I wanted it to look like a design collaboration between the minimalist architect Donald Judd and Karin Larsson at Sundborn. The result is this sofa.

Unfortunately, I don't have a library, so we put it in the hallway. Instead of lying there reading, we throw our coats on it and sit on it when putting our shoes on. Underneath the lid is plenty of storage space where you can store winter clothes, picnic blankets and Christmas tree lights.

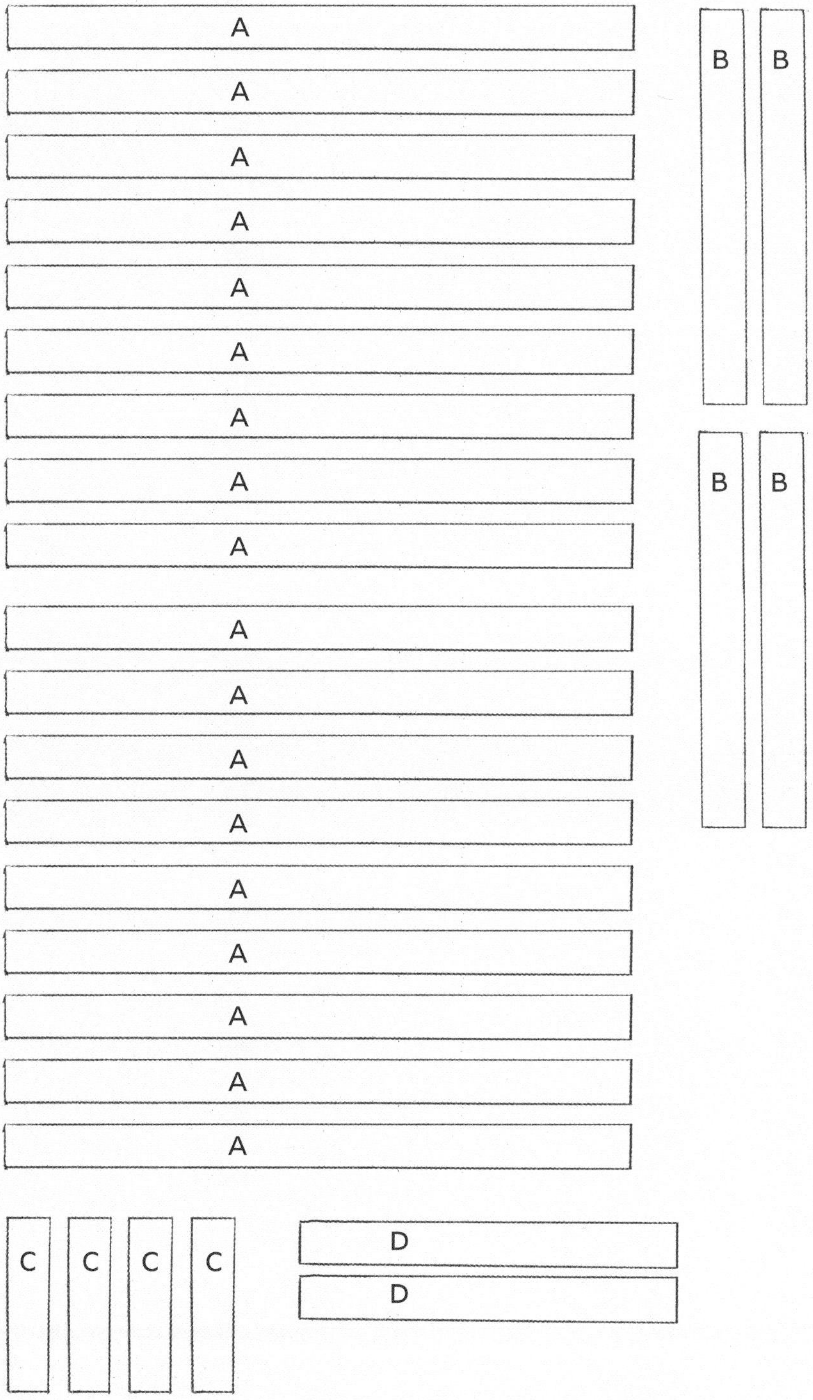

A

A

A

A

A

A

A

A

A

A

A

A

A

A

A

A

A

A

B

B

B

B

C C C C

D

D

Sofa

115

Furniture

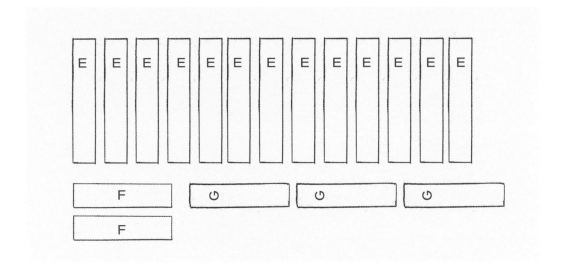

Piece	Dimension	Length	Quantity
A	95 × 21mm	1400mm	18
B	95 × 21mm	860mm	4
C	95 × 21mm	380mm	4
D	95 × 21mm	845mm	2
E	95 × 21mm	517mm	13
F	43 × 21mm	425mm	2
G	43 × 21mm	424mm	3

1. Start with the back: lay nine long A-boards out on the floor and join the two standing B-pieces along the sides. Fix into place with two angled B-pieces.

2. Assemble the front (four A- and four C-pieces) the same way.

3. Assemble the high side. Lay nine side boards (E) out completely straight on the floor. Fix into place with the long, angled D-pieces.

4. Stand the three finished sides up and assemble together by joining the high side to the outsides of the front and back sides.

5. Time for the low side: join the four remaining side boards (E) to the sides of the standing B- and C-boards. Start from the bottom, to make sure you get it straight.

6. Join the little bars (F) to the inside of the sides level with the top A-board at the front. They are there to act as supports for the lid to rest on.

7. Assemble the lid: lay five A-pieces out completely straight on the floor and join them together with the G-pieces, according to the plan.

8. Put the lid in place!

Front view

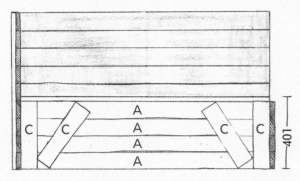

A
A
A
A

C C C C

401

Right side view

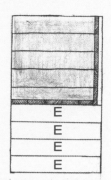

E
E
E
E

Back view

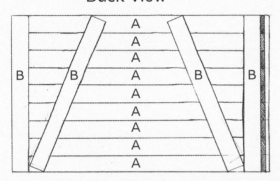

A
A
A
A
A
A
A
A
A

B B B B

Left side view

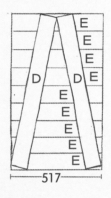

E
E
E
E

D D

E
E
E
E
E

517

Top view, without lid

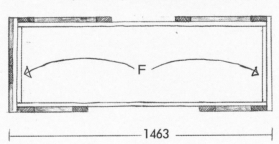

F

1463

Lid, underside

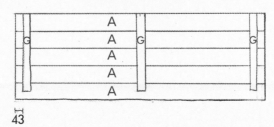

A
A
A
A
A

G G G

43

117

Top and tail bed

My two daughters like to sleep together but they are too young to climb up to a bunk bed. So I built this extended version of one of the beds that Enzo Mari designed for *Autoprogettazione?* It will take two children lengthwise. It sometimes happens that I doze off in it myself. To have that much space lengthwise as an adult is a luxury.

If you'd rather make one at standard length, you just shorten the A-pieces by 260mm and skip the G-pieces completely. Then it will be the right size for an 80 x 200cm-mattress. Since the sides of the bed are relatively low it is better suited to a simple foam mattress than a sprung mattress. The mattress designed for the Ikea Hemnes daybed is ideal.

If you want to save time and nails, you can replace the slats (H) with a finished slatted base 2000 x 800mm, for example Luröy from Ikea.

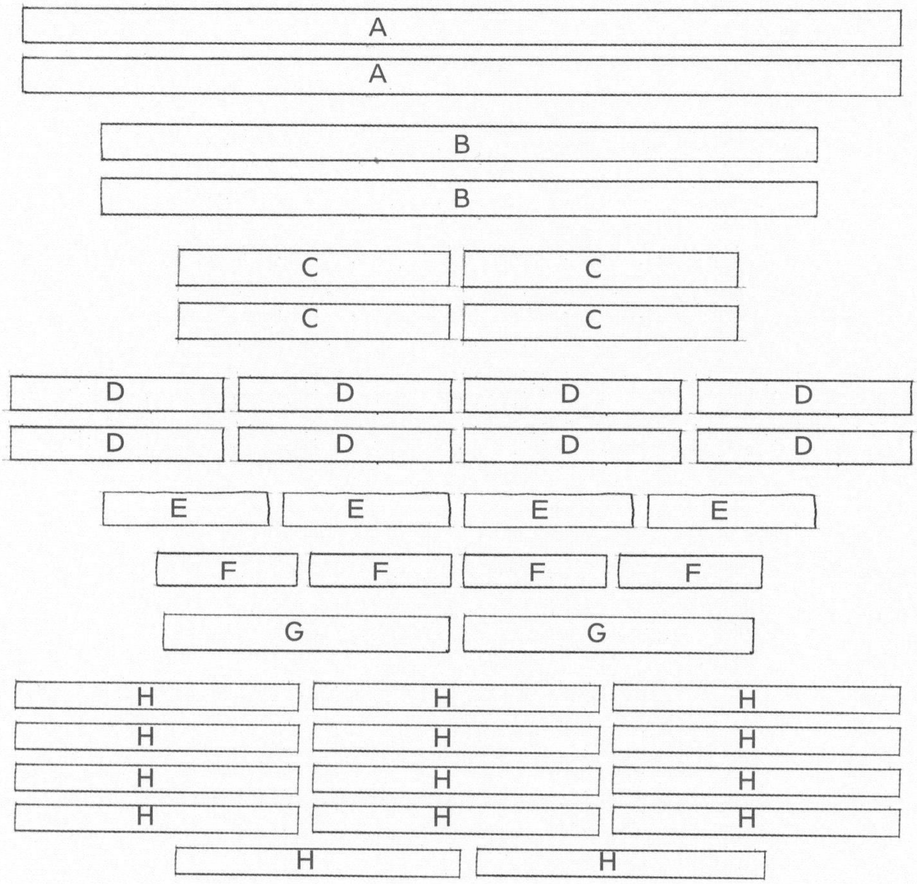

Piece	Dimension	Length	Quantity
A	95 × 21mm	2450mm	2
B	95 × 21mm	2000mm	2
C	95 × 21mm	758mm	4
D	95 × 21mm	600mm	8
E	95 × 21mm	470mm	4
F	95 × 21mm	390mm	4
G	95 × 21mm	800mm	2
H	70 × 8mm	800mm	14

1. Start with the short sides: join the top C-boards along the top of the legs (D). Nail or screw the bottom C-boards 210mm from the floor. Measure diagonally from corner to corner and adjust until the distances between the corners are equal. Fix into place with the F-pieces.

2. Next, join the remaining legs (D) to the outside of the assembled legs so that the sides, seen from above, form the shape of a shallow U.

3. For the long sides, join the B-boards in the middle of the inside of A so that they overlap by 21mm (see plan).

4. Join the long sides (AB) to the short sides, 210mm from the floor. When everything is straight fix with the E-pieces.

5. Now only the base remains: join the G-pieces nearest to the edge on each side of A, against the short sides. Next, put the slats (H) in place on top of B, evenly spaced. Start a few millimetres in from each side, 70mm is a good distance and then you can then use the slats to measure the gaps.

6. Buy a mattress that is – or that can be cut to – 2260 x 800mm.

Top view

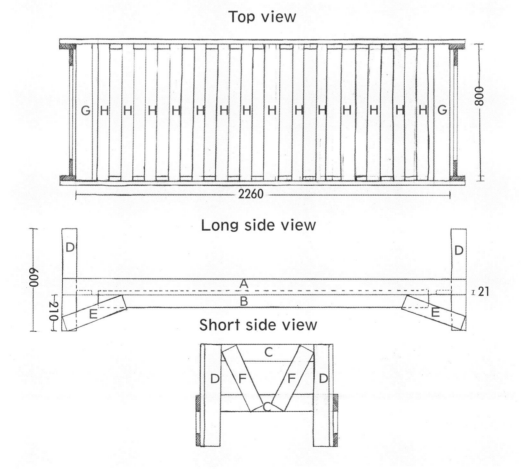

Long side view

Short side view

Dining table

I have adapted this construction, which is taken from Enzo Mari's *Autoprogettazione?* collection, so that you can sit three people on each long side and one on each short side without being too squashed.

The undercarriage looks neat, but it's a clever construction. The weight is distributed in a way that makes the table very sturdy, but at the same time you can sit anywhere without banging into the undercarriage with your knees. The tabletop's wide boards give a solid feel and allow the grain of the wood to shine through. If the table is being used as a dining table, I recommend treating the surface of the tabletop with linseed oil, for example, to protect it from stains.

For this project, it's a lot easier to use a screwdriver than nails and glue. Measure carefully! Few things are as annoying as a wobbly table. Since it does not have vertical legs in contact with the floor, this table is best suited for relatively even floors. And if it does wobble, it's easy to adjust afterwards.

Piece	Dimension	Length	Quantity
A	195 × 21mm	1800mm	5
B	43 × 21mm	970mm	6
C	43 × 21mm	700mm	6
D	43 × 21mm	1100mm	4
E	43 × 21mm	300mm	6
F	43 × 21mm	310mm	8
G	43 × 21mm	460mm	4

1. Start with one of the sides: join the bottom piece (C), centrally and across the bottom of the two legs (also C) so that the distance between the legs is 120mm.

2. Join a B-piece in the same way, but across the top of the legs.

3. Join the two E-pieces according to the plan. The distance between them should be exactly 300mm – so that the middle cross can slot in between them.

4. Measure diagonally from the two lower corners of the bottom piece (C) to the upper corner of the B-piece and adjust until the distances are equal. Fix into place with the F-pieces. If you have a spirit level, you can double-check that the B-piece is completely level.

5. Repeat step 1–4 to build the second side. It's a good idea to place the pieces on top of the finished side and use it as a template, to make sure they are identical.

6. Build the first middle cross: join an E-piece right across the middle between two D-pieces. Check the measurements from corner to corner to make sure it isn't wonky. Then fix with the G-pieces so that they are in contact with the E-piece in the middle. Then repeat everything in this step to make another middle cross.

7. Join the middle crosses to the outside of the legs, in between the E-pieces. The undercarriage is now complete.

8. Assemble the tabletop by laying the A-boards out onto your work surface. Remember to alternate the growth rings on the end grains so that every other board has a smiling mouth and every other has a sad mouth (see page 36). Assemble together with the remaining B-pieces.

9. Put the tabletop in place. When it is in the correct position you can join it to the undercarriage's standing B-pieces. If you think it's nice with nail heads you can nail from the top, but measure out carefully so that the nails are placed straight and evenly. If you don't want the joint to show, you can pre-drill and screw from the underside.

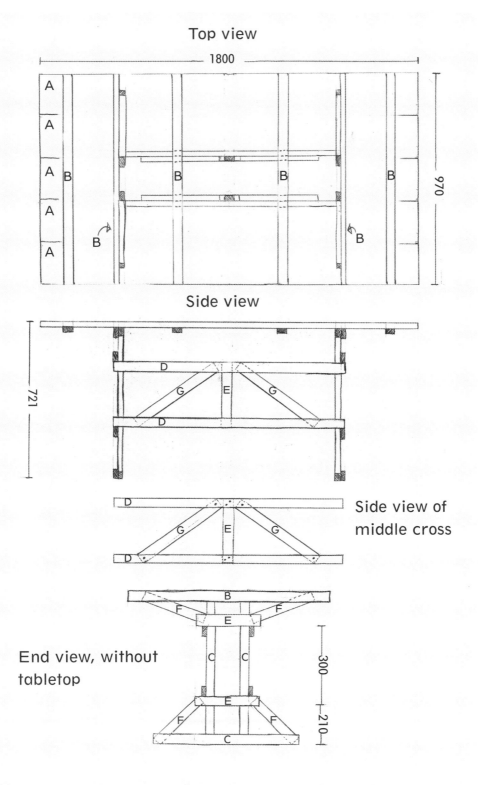

Top view

1800

970

A
A
A
A
A

B

B

B

B

B

B

B

Side view

721

D

G E G

D

Side view of
middle cross

D

G E G

D

End view, without
tabletop

B

F F

E

C C

E

F F

C

300

210

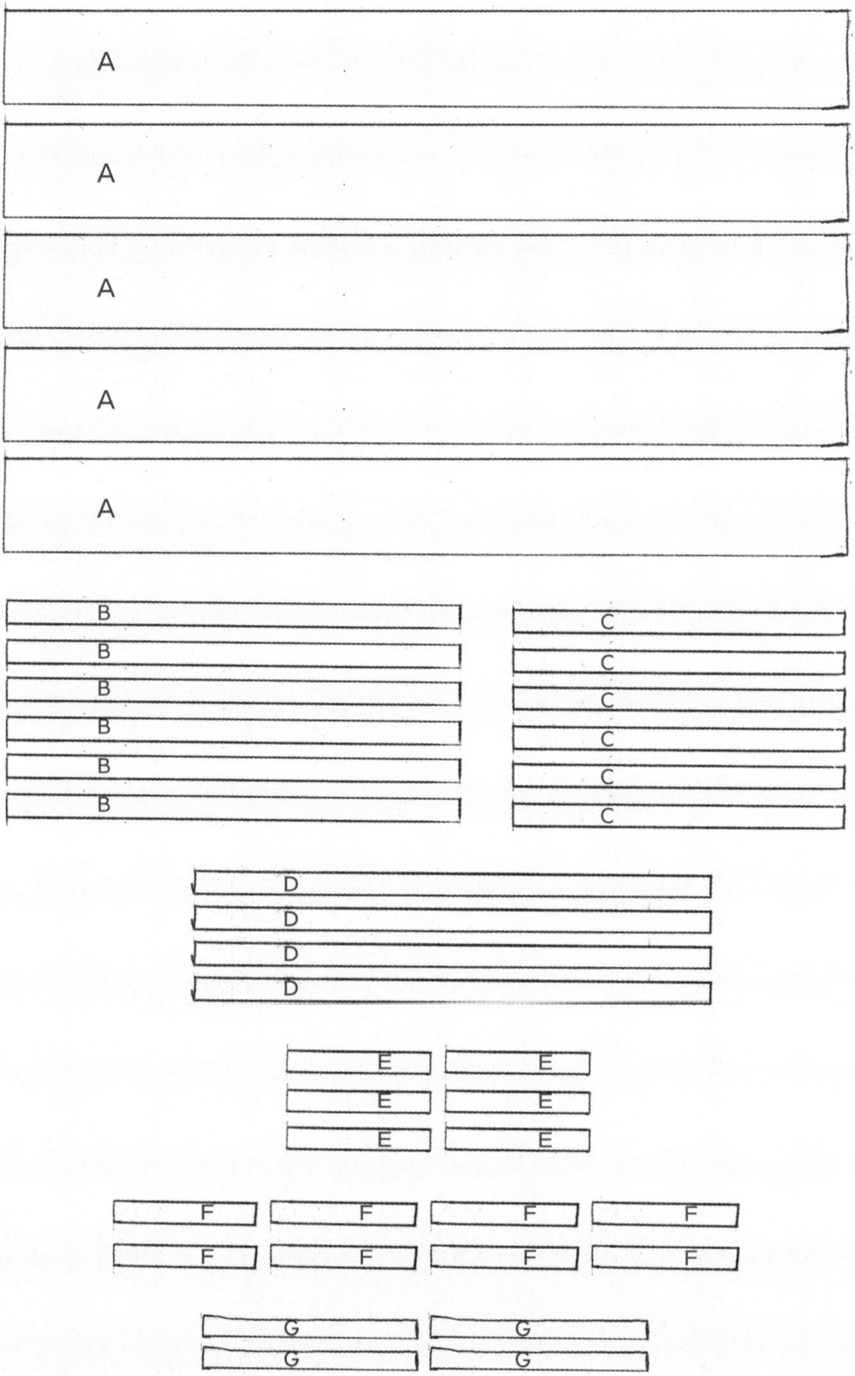

A

A

A

A

A

B

B

B

B

B

B

C

C

C

C

C

C

D

D

D

D

E | E

E | E

E | E

F | F | F | F

F | F | F | F

G | G

G | G

Worktable

I love the undercarriage on this table which is designed by Enzo Mari. There are no embellishments, each piece of timber has a supporting function. Yet, with its straight lines and shadows, it becomes a piece of art in itself.

You can of course use this table for what you want. But since the legs take up a lot of space it is better suited as a worktable or a desk than as a dining table.

Ours stands in the greenhouse where it serves as a planting table and work surface. I have therefore made the tabletop with 5–6mm gaps between the boards. If you want to use it as a desk you probably want the tabletop's boards to sit tighter. As a suggestion, you can in that case replace the plan's 8 A-pieces with 7 pieces of the dimension 118 x 21mm, and let the outer boards protrude 13mm on the long sides. If you want to use wider boards, you can use 5 pieces of the dimension 167 x 21mm and then this will leave an overhang of 17.5mm. Of course, you can also use thicker boards for the tabletop if you want.

Piece	Dimension	Length	Quantity
A	95 × 21mm	1440mm	8
B	43 × 21mm	1100mm	4
C	43 × 21mm	800mm	8
D	43 × 21mm	700mm	4
E	43 × 21mm	430mm	4
F	43 × 21mm	345mm	4
G	43 × 21mm	380mm	2
H	43 × 21mm	280mm	3

1. Start with the short sides: join the top edge of the legs (D) in between two of the C-pieces. It's good to use a square to make sure you get a right angle. Then assemble two more C-pieces 337mm from top edge of D. Measure diagonally from corner to corner and adjust the rectangle until the distances between the corners are equal. Then fix into place with the E-pieces.

2. Join the G-pieces between the long B-pieces, 21mm from the edge of the B-pieces. At the bottom edge, G should protrude 43mm. At the top, G should protrude 57mm. Join the H-pieces according to the plan. Measure diagonally between the outer corners and adjust so that the distances are equal. Then fix with the F-pieces.

3. If you tilt the middle strut you can insert it in between the sides' tilting E-pieces until G is in contact with C. Turn the middle strut straight so that it sits right in the middle of the lower C-piece and the top of G can be slotted in between the top C-pieces. Fix into place.

4. Lay the tabletop's boards (A) out over the undercarriage with a 5.7mm gap between each one. The outermost board should sit flush along the edge of C. Use a folding rule to position the screw or nail holes straight and evenly spaced and join the boards.

Top view

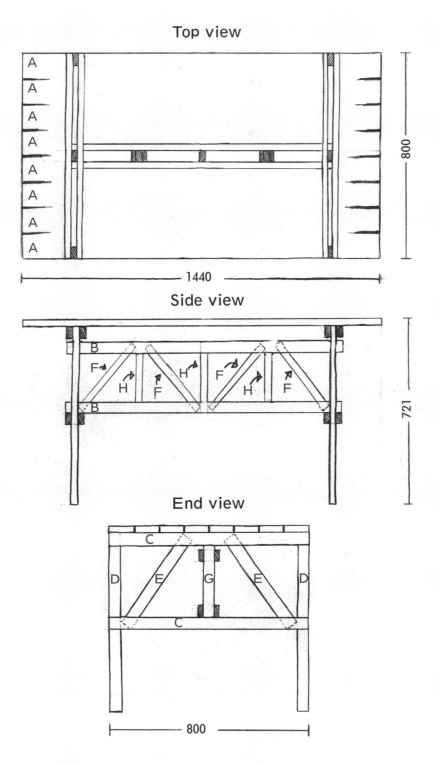

A
A
A
A
A
A
A
A

800

1440

Side view

B
F
H
H
F
H
F
H
F
B

721

End view

C
D
E
G
E
D
C

800

133

A
A
A
A
A
A
A
A

B		H
B		H
B		H
B		

C		E
C		E
C		E
C		E
C		
C		F
C		F
C		F
		F

D		G
D		G
D		
D		

Cabinet

This piece of furniture is also taken from Enzo Mari's *Autoprogettazione?* collection and is adapted to suit standard timber dimensions, although standards might differ depending on where you live. The plan shows an empty cabinet, but you can easily insert a shelf or a rail for hangers if you'd like. The depth of 60cm means that you will be able to put quite a lot of things inside.

The construction with the stabilizing diagonal brace is the same at the back as on the doors and so it looks just as nice freestanding in a room as it would against a wall. The construction is slightly more complicated than many of the other projects in this book: it requires working with large, thin sheets of plywood, which I recommend that you get cut to size at a hardware store or timber merchant. Make sure to choose decent-quality plywood and remember that the sheets of wood often have one nicer side that you should turn outwards. If you want to build a budget version you can replace the plywood with MDF or hardboard. It will contrast nicely with the light pine boards.

Each door will need two hinges and it's possible to mount them onto the inside or outside of the door depending on whether you want them to be invisible or more decorative. The instructions in step 19 are for mounting onto the inside of the door.

| A |
| A |
| A |
| A |

| B |
| B |

| C |
| C |
| C |
| C |

| D |
| D |
| D |
| D |
| D |
| D |
| D |

| E |
| E |
| E |

F	F	F
F	F	F
F	F

| G | G |

| H | H | H |
| H | H | H |

| I | I | I | I |

| J | J | J | J |
| J | J | J | J |

K

L

L

M

M

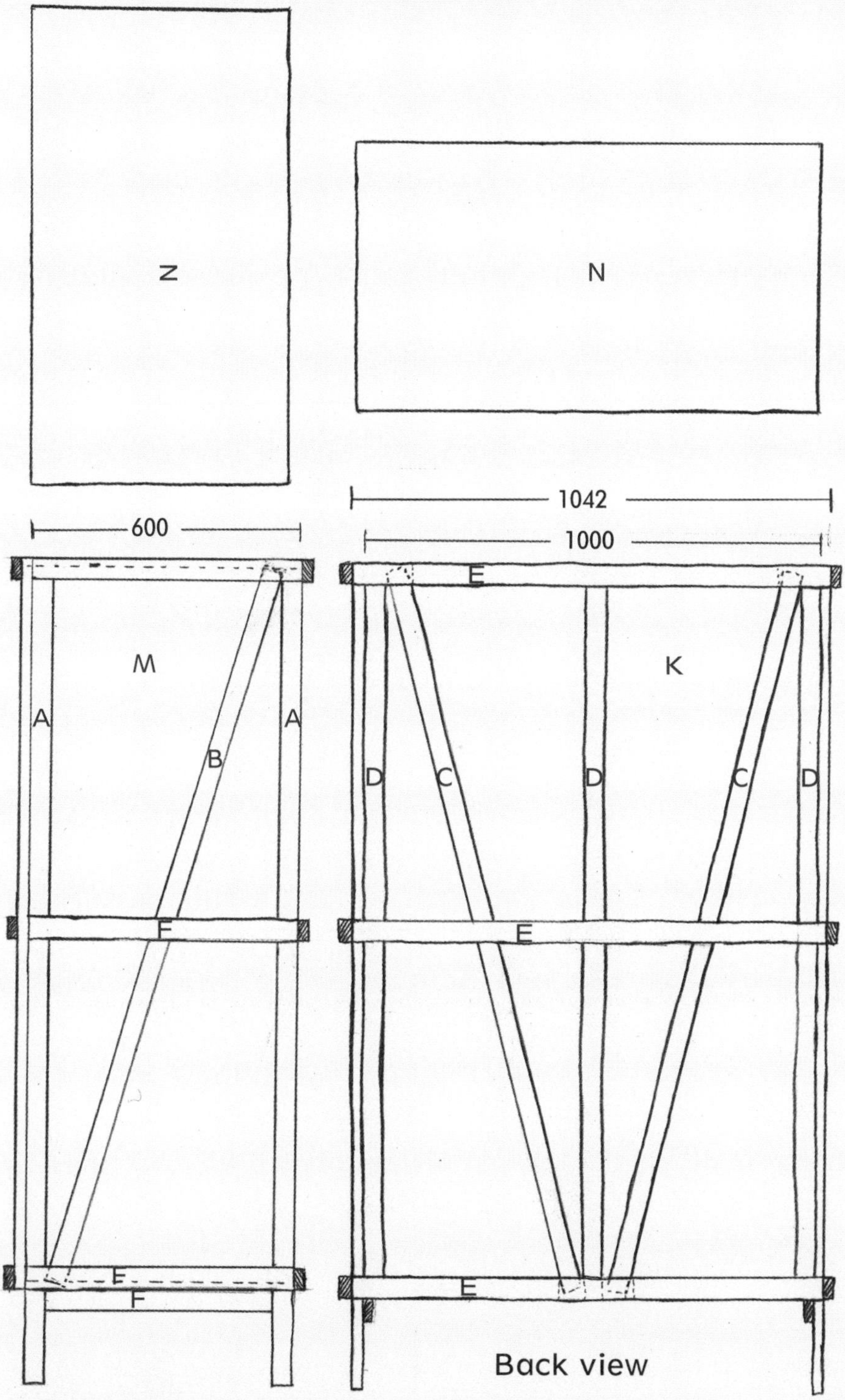

Z

N

140

1042

1000

600

M

K

A
A

B

D
C

D

C
D

E

E

E

F
F

E

Right side view

Back view

Top view

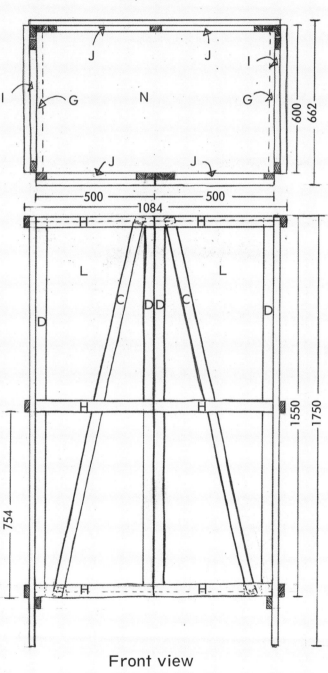

Front view

1. Start with one of the doors: join the D-pieces along the long sides of the L-sheet. Insert the screws or the nails from the back.

2. Join C so that it's tilting at an angle between the D-pieces.

3. Assemble the J-pieces at the bottom and top between C and D. (They should sit behind the top and bottom H-pieces on the plan.)

4. Join the doors' three H-pieces on top of the D-, C- and J-pieces according to the plan.

5. Repeat steps 1–4 to build the other door. Make sure to tilt C in the opposite direction. Be careful to put the handle (the middle H) at the exact same height as on the first door.

6. Assemble one of the sides: start by joining the A-pieces along the long sides of the M-sheet. They should be level at the top. At the bottom, the A-pieces will become the legs for the cabinet.

7. Join B so that it tilts at an angle between the A-pieces.

8. Put the I-pieces in place at the bottom and top between A and B (under F).

9. Join an F-piece in between the legs, so that its top edge is level with the bottom edge of the M-sheet.

10. Join three F-pieces to the outside of the A-, B- and I-pieces. Make sure that the middle is positioned at the same height as the door handles (H).

11. Repeat steps 6–10 to build the other side. Make sure to tilt B in the opposite direction.

12. Join the G-pieces to the insides of the sides, 18mm from the top. They should be flush against the front, but end 21mm from the sheet's edge at the back.

13. Assemble the back: join two D-pieces along the outer edges of the K-sheet, and one at the centre.

14. Join the C-pieces so that they tilt outwards from the middle D-piece.

15. Join the J-pieces at the top and at the bottom between the C-pieces and the middle D-piece. (J should sit behind E.)

16. Join the three E-pieces so that they protrude 21mm on both sides.

17. Join the base (N) to the sides' inner F-pieces and the top (N) to the G-boards.

18. Push the back in between the two sides and fix into place.

19. Fit the door hinges to the inside of M and L, making sure that they are also joined properly to A and D respectively.

Piece	Dimension	Length	Quantity
A	43 × 21mm	1750mm	4
B	43 × 21mm	1590mm	2
C	43 × 21mm	1565mm	4
D	43 × 21mm	1550mm	7
E	43 × 21mm	1042mm	3
F	43 × 21mm	600mm	8
G	43 × 21mm	575mm	2
H	43 × 21mm	500mm	6
I	43 × 21mm	465mm	4
J	43 × 21mm	365mm	8
K	plywood	1550 × 1000 × 4mm	1
L	plywood	1550 × 500 × 4mm	2
M	plywood	1550 × 600 × 4mm	2
N	particle board	1000 × 575 × 19mm	2

Gun Kessle's shelf

Ten years ago, I interviewed the then 84-year-old author Jan Myrdal in his cabin in Skinnskatteberg, Sweden. He lived on his own with his cat, felt forgotten and worried about what would happen to his kilometre-long book collection when he died. Most of it was stored in outbuildings on the grounds, but the books that he used the most he kept in his office, where a series of interlocked shelves in sun-yellowed pine covered the walls. I was fascinated by its simple but ingenious construction. You could easily extend it by adding new sections. The shelves could be moved without having to faff around with tools. Myrdal himself displayed a clear indifference to the design, but explained that his late wife, the artist Gun Kessle, had built it.

Soon after my visit the book collection was saved by the literature-loving billionaire Lasse Diding, who set up The Jan Myrdal Library and a new home for the author in Varberg. What happened to Gun Kessle's shelves I don't know, but several years later I saw a picture of a similar piece of furniture in an Italian book. Gun Kessle had apparently also been inspired by Enzo Mari.

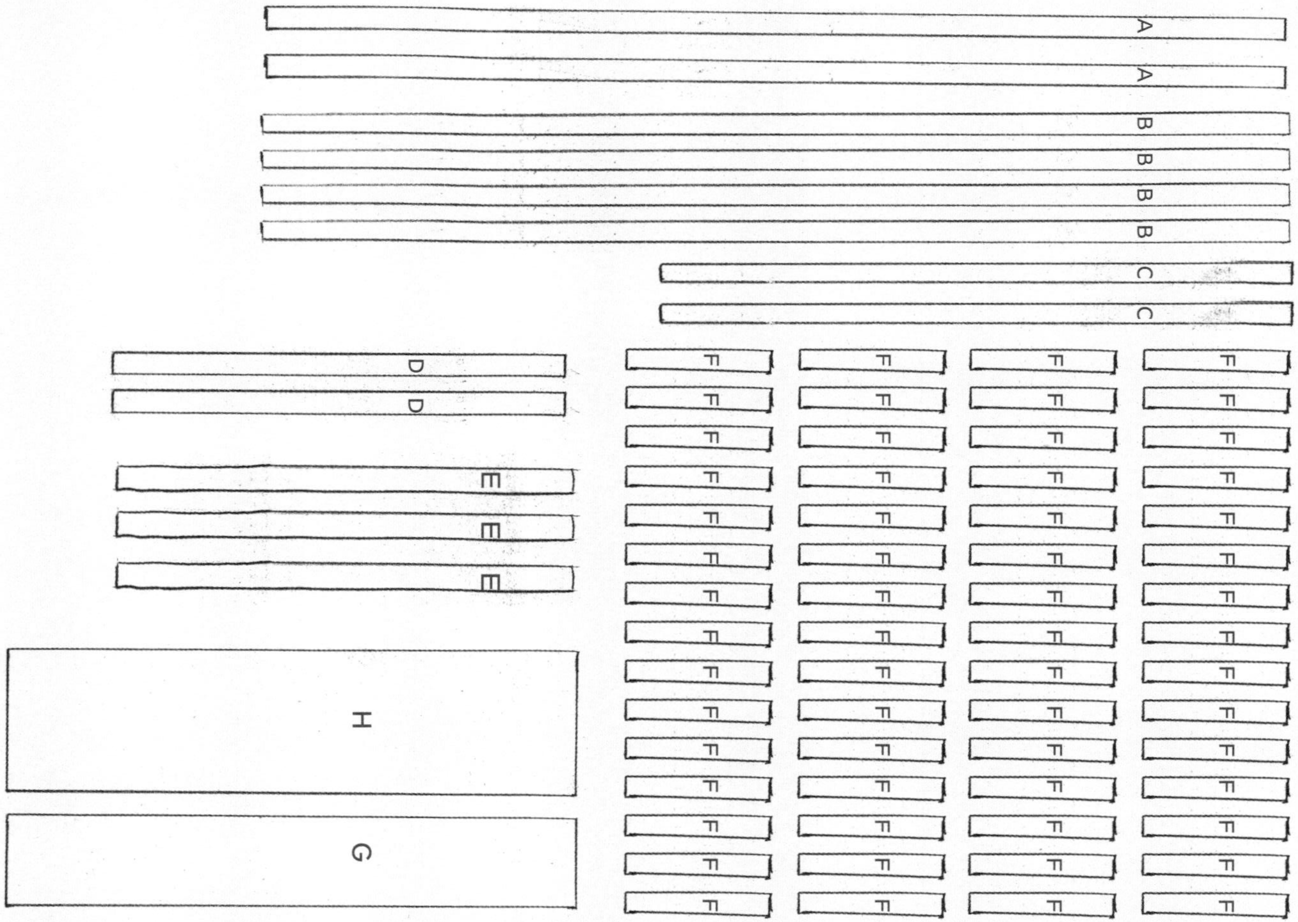

A A B B B B C C

F F F F F F F F F F F F F F

F F F F F F F F F F F F F F

F F F F F F F F F F F F F F

F F F F F F F F F F F F F F

D D E E E

H G

Side view   Front view

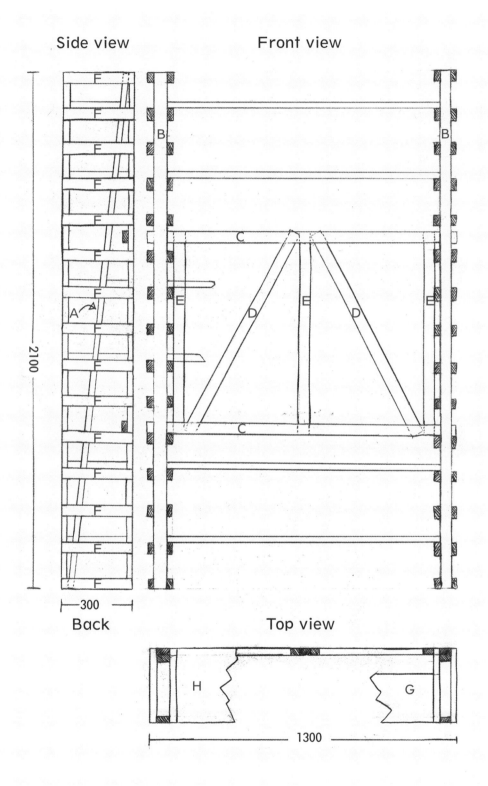

2100

F F F F F F F F F F F F F F

B   B

C   C

D   E   D

E   E

A

├── 300 ──┤

Back

Top view

H   G

├─────── 1300 ───────┤

Piece	Dimension	Length	Quantity
A	43 × 21mm	2110mm	2
B	43 × 21mm	2100mm	4
C	43 × 21mm	1300mm	2
D	43 × 21mm	930mm	2
E	43 × 21mm	835mm	3
F	43 × 21mm	300mm	60
G	195 × 21mm	1170mm	optional
H	300 × 21mm	1170mm	optional

1. Start with one of the sides: firstly, join one of the top and one of the bottom shelf supports (F) to two of the B-boards so that you get a rectangle. Then measure diagonally from corner to corner and adjust the rectangle until the distances between the corners are equal. Then fix the rectangle with the diagonal brace (A).

2. Join all the F shelf supports to one side of the rectangle. It's important that they are placed straight. In this plan, the distance between two shelf supports is 104mm. You can saw a 104mm long piece of wood to use for measuring. Start from the bottom and use a square to check that you place the shelf supports (F) straight.

3. Join the F shelf supports to the other side of the B boards. To find the exact same height as on the other side, you can place your measuring piece on top of the shelf supports that have already been joined.

4. Time to assemble the second side. Start by repeating the instructions in step 1.

5. Now you can use your finished side as a template. Place your new rectangle on top and make sure that you fix the shelf supports at the exact same height. If one piece is slightly narrower remember that it's at the top, where the shelves will sit, that they need to align.

6. Assemble the back brace (CDE): join E in the middle of both C-boards to form an H-shape. Join the two remaining E pieces. Measure diagonally from corner to corner and adjust until the distances between the corners are equal. Then fix the brace with the D-pieces.

7. Join the back brace (CDE) to the sides (FAB) so that they sit on any shelf support by joining C to B.

8. Put the shelves (G and H) in place. The shallower G-shelves are placed in front of the back brace.

9. If you want to extend the bookshelf, build one more side (FAB) and one more back brace (CDE) and add new shelves. Just keep in mind that the additional back brace cannot be placed at the same height as the first one. Secure the shelf to the wall to prevent it from tipping over.

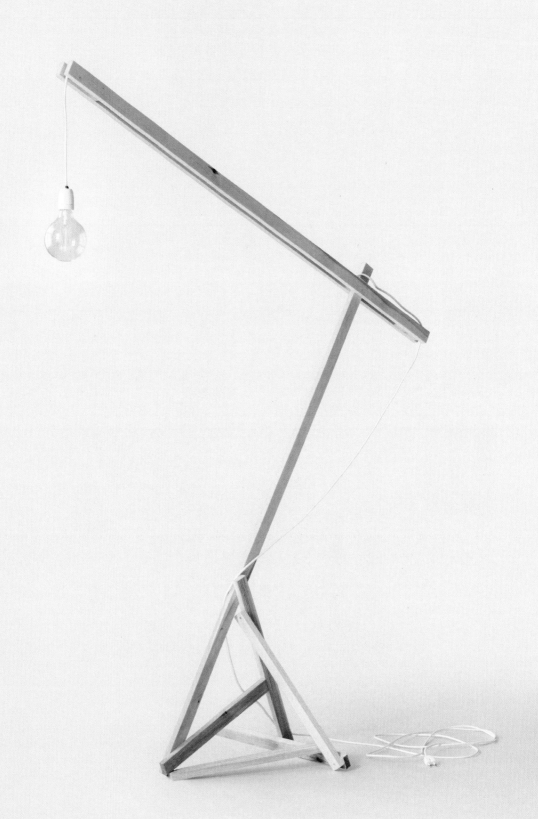

Giraffe lamp

Despite its slender body, this lamp takes up a relatively large floor space. If you have room for it, it will give a cosy light over a reading chair or a desk.

The lamp cord doesn't have to be secured into place anywhere. If it sits over both F-pieces and is wrapped around the top of the C-piece it will be hidden between the top arm's A-pieces and form a nice line hanging down to the base.

The pick-up-sticks-esque base is made from a handful of triangles that stabilize the tall, thin construction. It looks more complicated on the plan than it is in reality.

To make sure that it doesn't wobble I recommend that you use screws when assembling the base.

1. Start with the top arm: join the two A-pieces around the F-pieces, so that the latter sit 20mm from the outer edges of the A-pieces.

2. Assemble the base: screw one of the C-pieces into place outside B so that you get a 53-degree angle, 570mm from the bottom of the inside of B.

3. Screw the E-piece into place 230mm from the other end of the same C-piece so that is sits with the end grain against the narrow side of C.

4. Secure the other end of E to the inside of B to make the angles against the floor 67 and 60 degrees respectively according to the plan.

5. Join the other C-piece along the bottom of the C-piece in the triangle to form a T-shape.

6. Stabilize the base by joining G on top of the C-piece that sits against the floor and under E so that one of its corners sits against B.

7. Stand the base up. Stabilize B by joining D to both C-pieces, to create yet another triangle.

8. Insert the standing B-piece in between the two A pieces, so that approximately 300mm of one of the A-pieces protrudes behind B. Secure it so that 70mm of B protrudes at the top and you get an 85-degree angle underneath.

9. Hang the lamp cord over the F pieces so that it hangs down the required length. Wrap it once around the lower arm (B). Then wrap it around the top of the standing C-piece so that the cord hangs in a nice arch.

Piece	Dimension	Length	Quantity
A	43 × 21mm	1720mm	2
B	43 × 21mm	1780mm	1
C	43 × 21mm	620mm	2
D	43 × 21mm	565mm	1
E	43 × 21mm	480mm	1
F	43 × 21mm	120mm	2
G	43 × 21mm	535mm	1
H	Lamp cord	approx. 7000mm	1

Top arm section top view

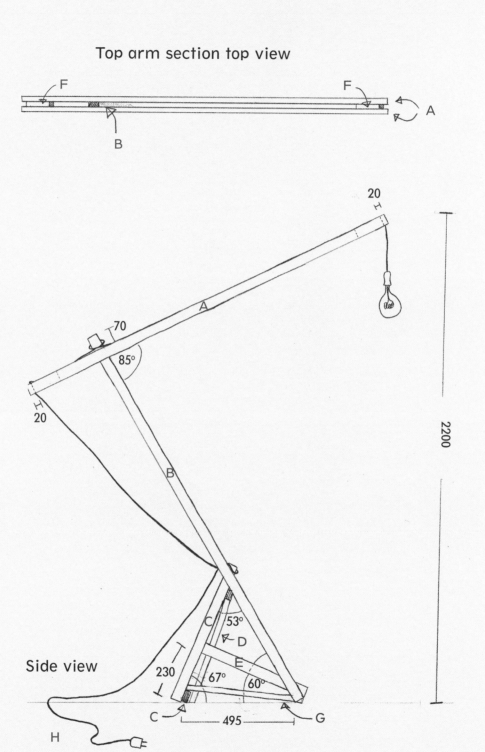

Side view

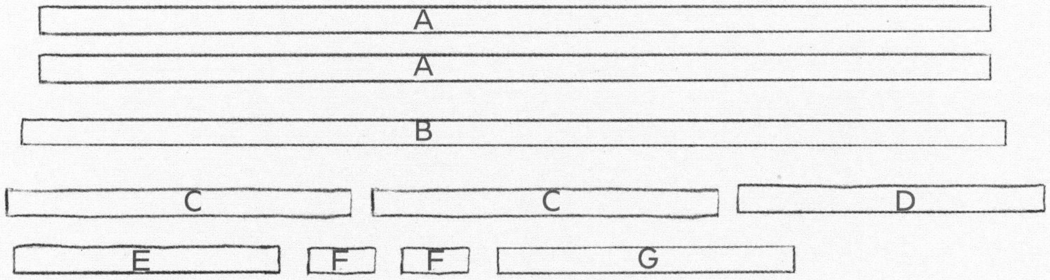

A

A

B

C

C

D

E

F F G

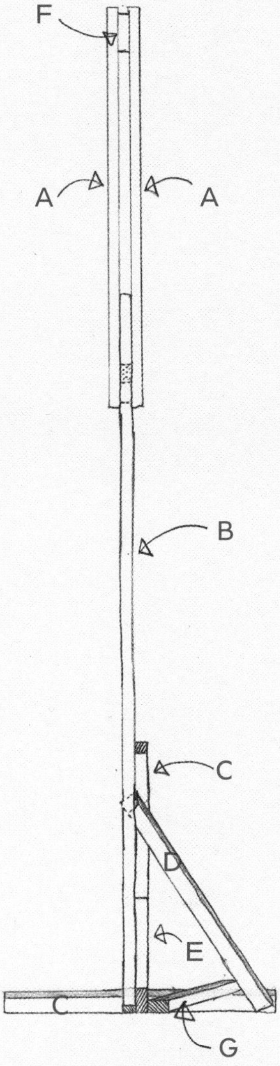

F

A A

B

C

D

E

C

G

Front view

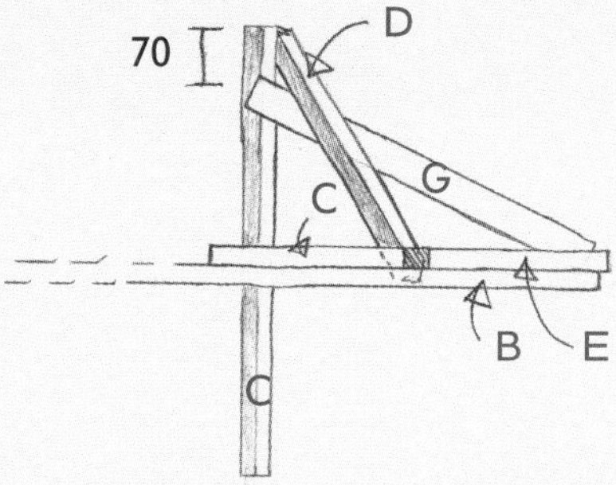

70

D

C

G

B

E

C

Base section top view

mm	in	mm	in	mm	in
4	1/6	337	13 1/4	610	24
5	1/5	340	13 3/8	620	24 2/5
5.7	2/9	350	13 7/9	640	25 1/5
10	2/5	360	14 1/6	650	25 3/5
13	1/2	365	14 3/8	671	26 3/7
15	3/5	370	14 4/7	690	27 1/6
17.5	2/3	380	15	700	27 5/9
18	5/7	385	15 1/6	750	29 1/2
19	3/4	388	15 2/7	758	29 5/6
20	7/9	390	15 3/8	760	29 8/9
21	5/6	400	15 3/4	800	31 1/2
22	7/8	405	16	810	31 8/9
30	1 1/6	408	16	835	32 7/8
35	1 3/8	410	16 1/7	845	33 1/4
40	1 4/7	415	16 1/3	850	33 4/9
43	1 5/7	420	16 5/9	860	33 5/7
50	2	424	16 5/7	930	36 5/8
57	2 1/4	425	16 3/4	970	38 1/5
60	2 3/8	429	16 8/9	998	39 2/7
70	2 3/4	430	16 8/9	1000	39 3/8
85	3 1/3	440	17 1/3	1042	41
95	3 3/4	441	17 3/8	1100	43 2/7
104	4	450	17 5/7	1170	46
118	4 5/8	460	18	1200	47 1/4
120	4 5/7	465	18 2/7	1200	47 1/4
125	4 8/9	467	18 3/8	1300	51 1/6
143	5 5/8	470	18 1/2	1316	51 4/5
145	5 5/7	475	18 5/7	1400	55 1/8
148.5	5 5/7	480	18 8/9	1440	56 5/7
150	5 8/9	481	18 8/9	1550	61
167	6 4/7	500	19 2/3	1565	61 5/8
195	7 2/3	505	19 7/8	1590	62 3/5
200	7 7/8	517	20 3/8	1600	63
210	8 1/4	520	20 1/2	1720	67 5/7
230	9	535	21	1750	68 8/9
250	9 5/6	540	21 1/4	1780	70
260	10 1/4	550	21 2/3	1800	70 7/8
270	10 5/8	565	22 1/4	2000	78 3/4
280	11	570	22 4/9	2100	82 2/3
300	11 4/5	575	22 5/8	2110	83
310	12 1/5	585	23	2450	96 4/9
330	13	600	23 5/8	7000	275 3/5

First published in the United Kingdom in 2022 by
Pavilion
43 Great Ormond Street
London
WC1N 3HZ

The chair on page 23 is Sedia 1 by Enzo Mari, photographed
by Jouko Lehtola, © Artek (www.artek.fi). The picture
on page 14 © Alamy Ltd. The adapted plans of the
Autoprogettazione furniture are used with permission from
the publisher Corraini. The other plans are by the author.
The author hopes that as many people as possible will build
the furniture in the book and even better, make their own
versions of them. Please send photographs of your projects
to ejealmqvist@gmail.com, or share them on social media
under the hashtag #hammerandnailfurniture. No plans can be
used for commercial purposes however.

ISBN 978-1-911663-90-4

A CIP catalogue record for this book is available
from the British Library.
10 9 8 7 6 5 4 3 2 1

Reproduction by JK Morris Productions, Sweden
Printed and bound by Toppan Leefung Ltd, China
www.pavilionbooks.com

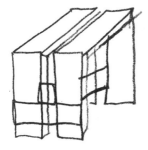